ABOUT THE AUTHOR

Brian Jones is a former Bank official, and independent Financial Adviser. Most of his adult life has been spent playing football and watching his beloved Wolverhampton Wanderers, as well as a cricket career spanning fifty-two unbroken years. After retiring from office work, he now delivers Bikeability to schoolchildren. Recreationally he is a racing cyclist, and is particularly active in Time Trials.

These days he lives in Surrey, cycling and singing in a church choir and a choral society.

His first book **'MISSPENT YOUTH'** recounted his formative years from 1950 to 1969 and the reasons why his adult life panned out the way it did, and not perhaps the way it should have.

'MISSPENT DOTAGE' chronicles his addiction to cycling when he reached the age of 57 weighing twenty two and a half stone and quickly became a racing cyclist.

MISSPENT DOTAGE

or Grey Racer

By BRIAN JONES

We all started somewhere Sean!

Yours in cycling

JANUARY 2021

PUBLISHED by BRIAN STUART JONES PUBLISHING

bsj219@outlook.com

DEDICATION

This book is dedicated to the bicycle, my constant inanimate companion. God bless the person who invented this wonderful machine, whoever you were, for not only has it given me immeasurable pleasure, but the health-giving benefits manifest themselves every morning when I awaken and look forward to another day in the saddle. Chapeau!

DISCLAIMER

This work depicts actual events in the life of the author as truthfully as recollection permits and/or can be verified by research. Occasionally, dialogue consistent with the character or nature of the person speaking has been supplemented. All persons within are actual individuals; there are no composite characters. I have intended no detriment to the characters of people still living, nor to those who have gone to a better place. The only person who has their character maligned in this book is the author himself.

ISBN no. 978-1-8380005-1-6

CONTENTS

FOREWORD

When Brian asked me to write the Foreword for "Misspent Dotage… or Grey Racer" I felt not only flattered, but a great sense of responsibility. As you will read, the bike to Brian is as essential to his being as bread and water is to everyone else. This book captures Brian's love affair with the cycle that only grows stronger with time.

I have had the great pleasure of meeting Brian through our cycle training activities and our shared love of racing push bikes!

I must say I find Brian a true inspiration. Not many riders will step off a bike after a cold, windy evening 10-mile Time Trial with a glint in their eye and a spring in their step as if they had just completed their first race!

And now through Brian's cycle training activity, he has gone full circle - teaching the next generation to ride bikes. For many this will give them a more informed knowledge of road craft and provide the confidence to make simple on road journeys to the shops. But for many others, I have no doubt, that the seeds Brian sows in their training may lead to their own memoirs, a book and love affairs with this enchanting machine that last their own lifetime.

Ed Clark

April 2020

INTRODUCTION

This could take some doing, but I am going to regale you with a story which has remained firmly engraved on my guilty conscience from the age of about five years old, because it involves me as the central character, and therefore the villain; awash with cruelty, so you, the reader, will hate me from the very first paragraph of this tome. Which in itself could be some sort of unwanted record. No one wants to read about a bully.

To set the scene let me beam you back to the mid-nineteen fifties, where you find me and my very first contraption on wheels, which was a lovely bright red and light blue tricycle, It had a boot that opened via a hinged lid inside which I would keep the most important of my toys. Being of but five years old as stated,

I was certainly not very athletic so I used to content myself by turning the pedals on my trike and riding up and down our entry. This led to the pavement at the front of the road where we lived in an end of terrace house. There was a row of seven houses, and our family occupied the one at the end of the terrace. It was a very pleasant setting where we lived in Bearwood, which I thought was the nicer end of Smethwick, this being a town historically in Staffordshire and is situated a mere four miles west of the centre of the city of Birmingham.

At the other end of the terraced houses lived a family who had a little boy who was approximately the same age as me, or perhaps a year younger. He had a similar trike to mine and his was coloured black, as I seem to recall. His name was Ronald and he was a lovely little chap, never doing me any harm whatsoever.

One day the two of us were out on the pavement with our trikes, completely unsupervised as no-one had heard of paedophilia then, so we were fine wiling away the time without adult supervision.

I bet you are wondering why you should be hating me after setting such an idyllic scene of life so long ago. Well, to my eternal shame, here it is.

Ronald was parked alongside me as we both sat astride our trikes, when with no provocation whatsoever, I dismounted from mine and going over to him, I tipped him backwards over the rear axle of his tricycle. His head hit the pavement with a resounding thump, and the front wheel of his trike was sticking up in the air. He cried out loudly, then he cried and cried and then cried some more.

I do not know to this day why I did this awful thing to him, but you know when you have those recurring nightmares which always centre on things you wish you hadn't done, then this incident still comes back to haunt me. I wish to this day I hadn't done it and I felt so, so sorry for Ronald and, if he is still with us, I hope he can find it in his heart to forgive me.

And if he has gone to meet his Maker, then I hope when we stand face to face with each other once more I can apologise with all my heart and seek his forgiveness. I am cringing with embarrassment and remorse even as I pen these words.

Shamefully, there it is, my first cycling, or bike-related recollection and it is a dreadful one. Now that you, the reader, hate me with a vengeance, please allow me to try and make up for this random act of cruelty by telling you the rest of my story, so that by the end of it you might like me. Perhaps, a little bit.

Fast forward to the present day, and I am a changed person. My love affair with the bike started in earnest on Saturday, 1st September 2007, a day which truly changed my life. I will explain in more detail as my story unfolds. I am now in my 70th year as I write these words, and my relationship with the bicycle, whilst perhaps not a love affair per se, can be more accurately defined in my view as akin to a blood relationship.

I am truly that close to my bikes, and it makes me feel quite emotional if, for example, I hear of someone, whom I have probably never met before in my life, suffers the misfortune of having their bike stolen.

To me that feels like a bereavement. Mistreat a bike and I feel its pain. To me a bike is a sibling, or a pet; and should be treated as such by its owner. This is my first attempt to make you, the reader, like me after that ghastly opening anecdote with which I have tried to gain your interest.

Cycling has saved and prolonged my life, that is an incontrovertible fact. When I had reached my mid-50s I weighed in at 22 and a half stones and without doubt this was rapidly shortening my life expectancy. From being morbidly obese at a dangerously vulnerable age, I have gone to someone who has never felt or looked fitter, having shed nine unwanted stones in the interim.

When I eventually meet my Maker, I hope he has a bicycle waiting for me, because riding around heaven is something I could get used to and will look forward to. But only when my time is up on this earthly cycle track.

ACKNOWLEDGMENTS

Special thanks again to Mary Bodfish, respected local historian and one of the leading lights of the Smethwick Heritage Society, for repeated her feat of proofreading 'MISSPENT DOTAGE' as she did with my first literary attempt 'MISSPENT YOUTH'.

Not only that she has also made the necessary adjustments to my grammar, punctuation and length of sentences in order to ensure that you, the reader, have as smooth a passage through this book as possible.

Without her this journey would have been far more difficult.

CHAPTER ONE

When I First Climbed into the Saddle

In my previous book "Misspent Youth" I set out my early relationship with the bicycle. I will briefly go over that story, and then build on it for you.

At the age of 11 I was preparing to finally leave Bearwood Road Primary School, which was in the town of Smethwick, Staffordshire, and was situated a mere half-mile walk from my home. I was to enter Holly Lodge County Grammar School for Boys, and this was at the other end of the town, and situated two-and-a-half miles from home as the crow flew.

My older brother Roger, who was six academic years ahead of me, had completed his time at the Lodge. Most of this he had not only spent cycling to and from school, but had combined it with a twice-daily newspaper delivery round, which he also accomplished on two wheels.

This led to him being supremely fit, and to his taking up the sport he loved above all other, cycling. He rode competitively on the track, or the velodrome, to give it its correct title. I, as the younger sibling, had watched his cycling career burgeon with considerable interest but without showing much inclination to follow in his footsteps (or should that be tyre tracks?).

However, my parents, who had also shown great interest in Roger's cycling career, had decided that the younger boy in their charge should also become a skilled cyclist. This led to them duly funding the purchase of new parts for a bike, which would be assembled by my brother for me to ride on to and from grammar school.

Fortuitously, Roger was also a knowledgeable self-taught bike mechanic, inheriting his engineering skills from my Dad, who was a skilled toolmaker in the aero-engine industry. Unfortunately, that ability chose not to be manifested in me and I remain, to this day, a comparative ignoramus when it comes to all things mechanical. Don't get my brother started on that particular topic!

He still says that I can ride a bike but haven't got the first idea how it works or fits together. (And his point is?) Mom and Dad always found the money from somewhere for this type of thing; we were never short of money as a family unit and neither did we borrow from anywhere, so we didn't owe anybody anything; and anyway, if I cycled to and from school then the saving in bus fares would soon repay the cost of the bike. Home economics *par excellence*!

This new bike was lovingly assembled by Roger during that summer of 1962. Before the school holidays were over it was unveiled to me in our back garden, leaning against the door of my Dad's garden shed, itself an engineer's treasure trove. We all looked on in awe at this beautiful, gleaming new machine.

Its centrepiece was a Viking frame in the most striking claret colour, and every component was brand new and shiny. It had gears too, although I hadn't the first idea what they were, what they did or how they worked. The handlebars were straight, making it a hybrid, as my parents, or Mom in particular, would not sanction the fitting of dropped handlebars, like on big brother's bike. Very prudent. All I had to do was get on it and ride it, which of course I did.

Now I can't remember how or when I first learnt to ride a bike, which is surprising as I can clearly recall how, when and where I learnt to swim. But I could already actually ride a bike when this Viking beauty passed into my possession, and so off I pedalled.

The ride to Holly Lodge was two and a half miles of busy, undulating roads, and I set off, following the path my brother had blazed so many years before me.

The trip was not easy. On the way to school, the major obstacle was the long drag of a climb up Thimblemill Road to its summit with the crossroads at William Road. This climb was tough for an unfit cyclist like me, but I learned to cope, and even got better at it as my muscles adjusted and cooperated.

Of course, the return journey meant that one whizzed down Thimblemill Road at breakneck speed, and then had to face an equally unpleasant uphill drag home. Some days it was quite easy in either direction, whereas other times it felt as though I was wading through treacle. I didn't realise it at the time, but this was due to the effect of the wind direction which would dictate whether or not the rides felt easier or simply plain tortuous.

Because we had a 90-minute lunch break at the Lodge, I sometimes rode home for lunch and then made my second journey of the day to and from school. You would think that this increased exposure to serious cycling would have made me fitter. You would be right.

But the winter of 1962-63, my first at the grammar school, was the worst in living memory, as it snowed heavily on Boxing Day and drifted to enormous heights. We then endured 10 weeks of sub-zero temperatures, which kept the frozen snowdrifts exactly where they had been created for the entirety of that period.

The long-awaited thaw set in finally during mid-March. Through all of this time that the Big Freeze held sway the roads had been palpably unfit for riding on safely, and my consequent inactivity on the bike meant that some sort of inertia had gripped me where cycling was concerned; and even after the weather improved I would catch the school bus as often as I could.

Mom and Dad didn't seem to mind, as I used the bike just often enough to make them think they hadn't wasted their money, and that I had come to dislike the bike. In truth two things happened as a result of the weeks of snowbound inactivity, in that I lost my place in the school football team, and stopped cycling regularly.

Therefore my weight, not for the first or last time in my life, started to increase.

One balmy evening during the following summer of 1963, I was out riding my Viking bike in Bearwood when I turned left off the main Bearwood Road into Rutland Road. I continued my journey riding in the head-down mode that I still inadvisably utilise, and promptly cycled straight into the back of a parked Volkswagen Beetle.

The impact sent the back wheel up into the air and I went careering over the handlebars, landing on the boot of the Beetle cheek first. (Before you ask, I refer to the cheek on my face!). I climbed to my feet, still groggy from the not inconsiderable impact, picked up my bike, and after giving it a quick once-over found nothing untoward with it, and so set off on the short journey home.

Some days later, when it was in its traditional resting place against the door of Dad's shed, my brother (who unbeknown to me had been born with x-ray bloody vision!) noticed that there was a severe kink where the crossbar met the stem. This had been caused on impact with the VW, but I think I lied by saying, when questioned by my brother, that I didn't know how this warp in the metal had got there.

To my horror, he declared that the bike, which believe me I cherished, was scrap as it was now unsafe to ride. After a sympathetic consultation with Mom and Dad, we all went to the local bike shop on the Bearwood Road run by Bob Mansell, a well-known local bike racer. With Roger's guidance we bought a brand-new hybrid bike, similar to my first, as Roger didn't have the time and probably the inclination to build another one from scratch, as he was now working full time at the Inland Revenue.

I can't remember the frame make of this bike, but it was a dark shiny orange colour and another very smart-looking machine. Roger filled me with joy as he intoned "And bloody well look after this one, unlike the last one!". What he meant was, own up if you smash it up you little (expletive deleted). And so this new bike became my school bike for whenever I didn't jump onto the school bus.

This pattern continued until my 14th birthday was approaching, and again, copying my brother's path, I underwent a medical with the County Borough of Smethwick Education Committee to give me the go-ahead, if I passed muster, to start a paper delivery round as soon as my birthday arrived. This, of course, meant I would be earning money to supplement my two existing sources of pocket money, which were my parents and my brother.

I was quite looking forward to this job, and on Monday, 23rd November 1964 (the day after my 14th birthday) I presented myself for duty at Riddell's Newsagents, on the Bearwood Road, near the King's Head junction of the Hagley Road, one of the main thoroughfares into the centre of Birmingham.

I was given a bag (naturally) and allocated a delivery round. Of course, it had to be one my brother had had before me. This comprised a half-mile ride into Harborne, one of Birmingham's most well-heeled suburbs, with its massive houses and affluent inhabitants. I duly delivered the Monday morning papers, and the Birmingham Mail during the evening round. This first week of my employment also coincided with exam week at school, and this was to pose a massive problem for me.

That first day the morning paper round took me ages. It was dark (and bloody freezing when I started at the ungodly hour of 6.45 a.m. at Riddell's), and my unfamiliarity with the addresses I was delivering to slowed me up. By the time I had got home, and Mom had insisted on me having a proper breakfast, I set off for school, again on my bike, thus arriving at school not only late for registration, but also for the start of that morning's exam, which was a heinous crime.

Any protestations about my paper round fell on deaf ears, and my form master warned me as to my future conduct with regard to my timekeeping; and I was shoehorned into the exam with a late start.

It didn't make much difference, as my exam performances that particular November were on the garbage side of abysmal.

Much, much worse was to follow the next morning, which of course was the Tuesday. I feel certain that all delivery boys from that era know what Tuesday meant; it was the day that the women's glossy magazines were published and they were to be delivered along with the Tuesday morning newspapers.

Ray Whittle, the paper shop owner Joe Riddell's son-in-law, ran the business in the mornings. He was to initiate me into the way of things to come, by showing me how to sort my own papers and magazines pre-delivery, so that effectively I was packing my own delivery bag.

Because my round in Harborne involved customers who had a bob or two, then every lady of the house seemed to have the three main publications of the time. These were the Woman, Woman's Weekly and Woman's Realm, all of them glossy and outrageously heavy. By the time my bag had been packed it not only weighed a ton, but stuck out halfway across the Bearwood Road, as I slung it over my right shoulder. Fate was determined to put me on a steep learning curve that morning, because it was cold, it was dark. and it was hosing down with rain in Biblical proportions.

My bike was standing upright against the kerb, and I walked towards it, or rather waddled, like a pregnant hippopotamus whose offspring was growing directly over its right hip. I prepared to swing my right leg over the crossbar, my standard method of mounting the bike. But I couldn't lift my leg off the floor, as it had been pinioned against my side by the sheer weight of the bag.

I reccied the situation, and decided that if I lifted the bag away from my hip to free my leg, then I could at least manhandle said appendage over the crossbar and on to the pedal on the other side of my bike. Which I attempted; with disastrous results.

My right leg went up in the air OK, but as it started to come down towards the other side of the bike, the weight of these confounded women's magazines meant that my whole body, and the bag to which I was attached, went with it; and gravity had it all crashing face down into the road. The papers which had been lovingly and carefully sorted by me shot out of the bag and formed a giant fan across the Bearwood Road, which was getting busier by the minute.

Those papers and magazines which weren't being torrentially rained upon also suffered the ignominy of being run over by the rush hour traffic. I was in a terrible predicament. Ray Whittle had watched this pantomime unfold with horror from within the shop, and he came rushing out; concerned not for the safety of me and my bike, but the apparent millions of pounds of his precious customers' newspapers and magazines which were rapidly being reduced to papier-mache!

We gathered up the contents of my delivery bag as quickly as possible, and tried to salvage what we could from the debris, but there was one hell of a lot of newsprint which needed replacing that morning. I am not sure if Ray ever forgave me for all of that, but I like to think that I repaid him by serving his paper shop loyally for three years.

When I got home, I discovered the horrendous weight of that Tuesday morning delivery bag had left huge red wheals in my upper torso which took ages to heal. Needless to say, I was late again for school that morning. I think I was placed in detention, from which I received a reprieve due to an appropriate missive penned by my Mom, citing my paper round as the root cause of my repeated tardiness. If she hadn't written that letter, I would have written it myself, because fate had decreed that her handwriting was as near as dammit identical to my own!

I did recover from that horrendous baptism of fire to become a super-efficient employee of Riddell's, even though I say it myself. Using my bike, I could complete a delivery round at breakneck speed, and my target became to deliver to every house on my route without stopping or dismounting from the bike. This was achievable because the houses in my Harborne round were all big with double-entry driveways, which enabled me to ride in one entrance, launch the bundle of papers at the front porch whilst on the move, and exit through the other gateway. Of course, my ever-increasing fitness levels helped me with this outrageous mode of delivery.

The other benefit of having such affluent customers came at Christmas time, when the tips I received were vast sums of money for someone as young as me. Envelopes containing Christmas cards with as much as 10 pounds inserted were not out of the ordinary. A tenner represented five or six weeks' basic pay from Riddell's, so these were riches indeed.

I remember my brother telling me that when he was a paper boy he was offered half a crown (12.5p in decimal currency) as a tip by the lady of some massive house and he refused it, on the grounds that the amount proffered was insulting, giving it back to her with the words "No thanks luv, you need it more than me!" Bravado of the highest order!

I carried on with my paper round until I was 17, but with sport taking over my life, then my Dad would replace me on my delivery round more and more often on the days when playing for the school football or cricket teams prevented me from turning up at Riddell's. My cycling activities became virtually non-existent.

Dad even let me sleep in on Sunday mornings if I had played two games of football on the preceding day so that I could recover properly. He would simply turn up at Riddell's, have a chat with Ray Whittle, with whom he got on enormously well, and deliver the Sunday papers using his car; sometimes with Mom accompanying him.

And from that point in history to that momentous day on the first day of September in the year of our Lord 2007 I didn't really trouble any bike at all.

CHAPTER TWO

I Become a Cyclist

I have two children, in order of naissance, a boy and a girl. Naturally I bought them bikes as part of their upbringing. I have always believed that all children should learn to ride a bike, and learn to swim, and be encouraged to develop those essential life skills. To accompany them on their rides when they reached secondary school age, I bought myself a nondescript hybrid bike from Halfords (other bike shops are available) but I never really got it out of the garage much, as my children showed very little inclination in riding their own machines.

However, some years later I booked a holiday in Brittany, north-west France and was due to arrive there on Saturday 1st September 2007 (that day again!). For some reason I attached my hybrid bike onto the boot of the car to take with me for the onward journey, on a bike rack I had been given by a neighbour for nothing (a surprising and very generous gesture). Please allow me to digress a little here and go back through my health history.

At school my weight yo-yoed alarmingly. Some years I would be a fat little lump, then other years this excess avoirdupois would all have fallen off me.

I would estimate that between the ages of 12 and 14 I was overweight, then from 15 to 18 I was slim and fit. This continued into my early twenties. I smoked a few cigarettes from the age of 18 onwards and drank a few beers, which did nothing for my calorie intake. I even joined a local Weight Watchers group which I found inspiring, but also a little daunting as I was the only bloke tipping the scales at these weekly showdowns so, as I have always thought of myself as a man's man, I decided to eventually give it a miss.

Let's face it, I couldn't really enter into any discussions about low calorie recipes and how to produce beneficial meals from them out of sheer embarrassment. Didn't really want to don a pinny in front of a group of women, however understanding and sympathetic they were. I know that this is not the stance to take in these days of emancipated enlightenment, but when did political correctness actually defeat bashfulness?

In my late twenties I bulked up again, and decided to do something about it as I got into my thirties. So I took up jogging, and I started pounding the streets. I actually became quite good at this, but I was in and out with it, so as soon as I stopped jogging (and it didn't take much to break my resolve), then my weight ballooned. I always seemed to be playing catch-up, because when I started jogging in earnest it was always to try and shed the pounds that I had put on during my latest spell of inertia (aka bone-idleness).

The Wolverhampton Marathon was to take place on the penultimate Sunday of March in 1984. I was thoroughly cheesed off with my physical condition after the usual Christmas excesses, and so I made a New Year resolution to start training for the Wolves Marathon and on New Year's Day off I duly went!

It was freezing and dark most of the time, so with a few layers on I started pounding the pavements. The difference was this time I had a purpose and I discovered I had within me a resolve I never realised I possessed.

As my mileage increased, so my speed improved, and my weight started to plummet. So much so that, not only was I back wearing clothes I couldn't get into post-Christmas, but I was having to buy new clothes as my waist size was reducing dramatically.

Despite the ravages of the cold, dark and damp winter my mileage continued to increase. 8-mile runs which had become my norm were being dwarfed by double figure mileages, and with the frequent company of my team mates Dave and Nige from Harborne Cricket

Club, a couple of Sunday mornings nearer to the big day saw two 16-milers successfully attempted.

I was working for Barclays Bank at this time actually in Wolverhampton itself, and one of the Assistant Managers asked me if I would obtain sponsorship for the local Round Table in order to raise a sum for charity. I duly agreed, which meant that if I backed out now, I would seriously lose face at work.

A number of people had told me that I couldn't possibly run under 4 hours on less than three months' training. I thought that I would give it a bash to try and make them eat their predictions, but it would be very difficult.

Come the day of the big race, there was something like six or seven thousand runners lining up. We all set off, and I started to jog and get into my rhythm. The miles started to click by, not with any great haste. I found myself at one stage in the company of Jimmy Savile, who at the time was high profile, and I noticed that he was encircled by a group of his minders so you couldn't get near him, even if you wanted to, which I didn't. I actually remarked after the race that there was something odd about his situation within the race, and I was glad when I lost touch with him during the proceedings. Little did we know!

Anyway, moving on, I went through the 20-mile mark in about 2 hours 40 minutes, equivalent to 8-minute miles, and my rhythm felt good. Doing a quick mental calculation, I had about 80 minutes in hand to run the remaining six-and-a-bit miles to get under my target time of 4 hours.

I thought "We're on here!", and I steeled myself to complete the job. Despite an uphill finish, I was lifted by the many thousands of spectators who lined the route, and their inspiration got me home in 3 hours 33 minutes 45 seconds. That officially made me a runner and not a jogger, as anything under 8-minute miles means you are a runner, according to the unofficial classification in the sport.

I was totally elated, but then discovered I couldn't walk at all for the next two days, with the severity of the muscle stiffness I was enduring. But then, miraculously on the third day, I went out and ran (not jogged!) a personal best for 10 miles. I was as fit as a butcher's dog and skinny as a rake.

The following year, after I ran the Wolverhampton Marathon, I had developed a rather disciplined habit of running during my lunch hour at the bank. This was made even more useful, in that I was managing a sub-branch of Barclays Bank in Waterloo Road, Wolverhampton, at the other end of the road from the Wolves home ground at Molineux. The rest of the staff was made up entirely of women. The branch had two toilet areas, one being palatial, and the other not so.

Yes, I pulled rank and claimed the palatial one, leaving the 10 or so women to share the smaller facility. This meant that I could change with total freedom in the vast area of space on which I had claimed squatter's rights, and get myself out to do one circuit of West Park before making my way back, without having inconvenienced any other member of staff.

One hot summer's day, however, in August 1985 I was jogging back to the office when I reached the multi-lane traffic light section of Waterloo Road where it meets the Ringway. As I was about to set foot onto the three-lane section, the traffic lights changed, and not in my favour; but I pressed on regardless.

I glanced to my right, and as I did a car came screaming across my path, catching me a glancing blow just above the right knee and sending me spiralling into the air.

I came back to terra cotta with a sickening thud and lay there, dazed, and in pain. (That should be terra firma shouldn't it?). Moving on . . . As it was a hot day, there were office workers looking out of open windows whilst devouring their lunches. One woman, who had seen the whole show, yelled at me to stay put, adding that she used to be a nurse.

Very soon a crowd had gathered round me, and the ex-nurse, when she arrived, decided that I might have broken my right leg. An ambulance arrived, and spirited me away to the local Accident and Emergency unit where I was treated.

After the hospital staff had taken my details it occurred to someone to let my office, that is, the bank, know why I had not returned from my lunch time activity. So a phone call was duly made, and they were informed of the silly thing I had got myself involved in. "Oh, we didn't know he hadn't come back from lunch" came their dispiriting rejoinder, and that was because I always got changed in my palatial "boudoir" and hadn't been missed! These things come back to bite you, don't they?

Remarkably, no X-ray was taken of my leg at the hospital. Some two weeks later when even the weight of a light bedsheet lying on my injured limb was causing me agony, I was forced to go to my own GP, who commissioned a hospital X-ray immediately. A fracture of the fibula, the non-weight bearing bone in the lower leg was diagnosed.

To add insult to injury, that day when I returned home, I sat down in the garden to rest my broken body and was stung on the arse by a wasp. Sometimes it just isn't your day, is it?

There were more periods of inertia (aka bone-idleness) to overcome in the immediate years and months following, although I did start the Wolverhampton Marathon again in 1996 after buying and training indoors on a wooden treadmill from Homebase or B&Q. It seemed to consist of rows and rows of cotton reels on skewers, but this noisy contraption enabled me to train without worrying about the wintry conditions outside, and I twice ran for 3 and a half hours non-stop as I tried to simulate a Marathon time and distance.

In the actual race itself I accidentally trod in a drain at about nine miles, spraining my ankle. With the injury swelling up I managed, with a combination of walking and gentle jogging, to get to the finish line during a snowstorm whilst dressed unfortunately only in vest and shorts. I was blue with cold as well as injured and my time of 5 hours 1 minute was disappointing to say the least. I was nowhere near as fit as I had been two years earlier.

Then I managed something else momentous, because on the 2nd of December 1987 I smoked my last cigarette. This was due to the facts that I could not afford the habit any longer; and, I reasoned, it would surely bring a premature end to my life just as it was instrumental in my Dad's early demise, This had definitely been attributed to the deadly weed.

Of course, the downside to this was that the weight piled back on, until I looked like a different person in photos taken of me from that time. The only saving grace was that, if I continued to play squash with Dave from the cricket club, and coupled that with some serious jogging, my weight would come down. But if I did no supplementary training then even squash couldn't prevent me from looking like an inflatable toy.

This annoying pattern went on year after year. My lack of resolve saw me assault the scales on the worst day at some 22-and-a- half stones, exactly twice the weight I had been when I crossed the finish line at the Wolverhampton Marathon. I was killing myself, and I thought that I would finish myself off before I even reached my Dad's age when he left us, at 55 years, 9 months and 7 days.

My brother, nearly six years older than me had rung me on the day he surpassed Dad's life span and boy, did he sound relieved! I actually got past Dad on the 30th August 2006, but it was around that date I was threatening to go through the floorboards if I got much heavier, or just plainly and simply explode through my calorific intake. Inwardly I said to myself that enough was enough, and I really had to do something to arrest what could easily become an irreversible, terminal decline.

Which brings us back (About time, I hear you cry!) to me unloading my hybrid bike off the back of my car in a tiny little Breton hamlet on that first September day of 2007.

I thought, well, if I have brought the bike all this way, then I had better get on it and ride the damn thing. So I climbed on and started pedalling.

And at that very moment my life changed forever and for the better.

The temperature was hovering in the low thirties, and the sun was unbearably hot, but I actually got the machine moving in a forward direction.

The rural lane ahead of me undulated a little, and I was trying to take in the idyllic French countryside, when after what seemed an eternity but was in fact two miles, I reached a little town. It was Saturday afternoon, but there was not a soul to be seen on its sun-baked main street as I pressed on.

The French road beneath my wheels was as smooth as a snooker table, and it was an absolute joy to ride on it as I kept going. After some more pedalling I calculated that I had ridden five miles, which felt as though I had just won a stage of the Tour de France; so I turned and began to retrace my tyre tracks. It was no easier on the return journey in the searing heat of the relentless sunshine that glorious afternoon, but I reached journey's end and contemplated what I had just achieved.

I had actually ridden 10 miles!

What a buzz I felt, and I resolved that if I could still feel my legs tomorrow, then I would damn well go out and repeat the feat. I could and I did! Making a mental note that I had now accumulated a total mileage of 20 miles, there was the genesis of a bug inside me. The third day I varied my route, encountering more in the way of uphill riding, which I found a little difficult, but I was actually feeling as though a few pounds were started to be sweated off.

I had my diary in my possession so I started to log the miles I had ridden that day and began a cumulative total.

My Halfords hybrid was at last starting to earn its corn, although the fact that it hadn't previously was down entirely to my laziness, inertia (aka bone-idleness), call it what you will.

Each day now began to revolve about getting my daily ride done and dusted, and thoughts during the day would turn to where I would make the bike take me next. One day I rode to the nearest big town which was some 25 miles away. This particular sortie took me well over two hours, but I made it and then got a lift back in the car.

At the end of the fortnight's holiday I had ridden 200 miles, all logged and totted up in my diary. I was living in Cardiff at the time, so when I returned home I immediately got the hybrid out again, and started cycling around the busy streets. At the end of that first month of September 2007 I had ridden and logged 452 miles, a Herculean effort. I was hooked and no mistake. It all felt the way it used to when I was jogging and training for races; do the effort, log it, total it all up then plan for tomorrow.

October dawned and I pedalled on regardless. My body shape was now starting to transform, and I was losing weight dramatically. During this second month I borrowed my son's dropped handlebar road bike as he wasn't using it much, and I continued riding merrily until one evening, in the dark (even though I had lights on the bike) I was cycling through the student area near to the University Teaching Hospital.

This locality had loads of students driving cars, and the Highway Code was not high on the priorities of many of them. I went to turn right into a side street, and the young schmuck driving the car coming towards me chose to ignore my chosen path completely and collided with me, dumping me and the road bike in an unholy mess on the ground. I think I was more badly injured than the bike, so after exchanging pleasantries with the now apologetic idiot who had been driving the car, set off to walk the half-mile or so home.

This was my first setback, and boy, was I sore. Badly bruised maybe, but inwardly there was a determination to get back on the bike as soon as possible.

The bike needed only a minor repair, which was duly accomplished, so with probably no more than a day or two's hiatus, my aching limbs found themselves back in the saddle again.

That second month of October saw me up my mileage, and I rounded up the two months' cumulative mileage to exactly 1,000. That was a considerable achievement, and one that I am still, to this day, proud of.

November, my birthday month, lived up to its reputation with its usual grizzly self – bringing bucketloads of miserable wet and cold weather, so I found myself making more frequent visits to the bike shops to supplement my growing wardrobe of cycling gear.

I was telling myself that maybe, just maybe, I had found some permanent good-living solutions with my daily cycling routine. My weight was coming down rapidly, and ergo so must my blood pressure. My inner organs must also be functioning much better, if not to say properly, as my lungs were being filled with God's own fresh air. Day-to-day inconveniences like headaches had also stopped bothering me. In short, I was feeling like a million dollars.

CHAPTER THREE

Cycle Mechanic (not!)

I have stated elsewhere in this book that my brother Roger has often said that I can ride a bike, but that I do not possess the first idea how to maintain or repair these machines; to paraphrase his rather more strident view on the subject!

That statement was made circa 1964 and rings almost as true today as it did then. Almost. I would love to have it on record that my early attempts at bike maintenance were comical, but they weren't. Simply due to the fact that were no attempts at bike maintenance by me.

It isn't that I wasn't interested, it is just that I had an older brother who could do it all for me, and he did. I could have learned by watching him, but I didn't. If I had a puncture, he fixed it. It was as straight-forward as that.

Roger built my first bike from scratch by buying new parts with the money Mom and Dad gave him for the purpose and he built a beautiful machine. It looked good, smelt brand new and was beautiful to ride. Please don't get me wrong, I was grateful to my parents and to my brother and I loved that bike, being really proud of it.

I have already mentioned the following incident in an earlier chapter, so please forgive me while we briefly re-examine the facts. One day I rode into the back of a parked car because I hadn't seen it ahead of me, due to my habit of riding with my head down. I went over the handlebars and hit, face first, the boot cover of the Volkswagen Beetle with which I had collided.

Both bike and I landed in an almighty heap on the ground, and I was, incredibly, unhurt. I picked myself up, then I picked my bike up, and quite normally rode it home. As the bike got me home without any problem, I naturally assumed that it had survived the collision unscathed. So I thought no more about it; and certainly didn't mention the incident to anyone in my family. How wrong could I be?

I used to lean the bike against the door of my Dad's wooden garden shed, which presented the bike fully side on if you were looking out of the sitting room window. My eagle-eyed brother thought that something didn't look quite right about my bike, so he wandered out to have a look at it from close quarters.

Sure enough, the crossbar tube where it met the stem had a kink in it, which could only have been caused by the concertina effect of the collision. Curious as to how this had occurred, he enquired of me, the rider of said bike, as to what had caused the aforementioned kink in the crossbar tube.

"I don't know" I lied unconvincingly, and my brother opined that I must have had some sort of collision with an immovable object. "Nah, don't think so," I continued to fib, although not quite as confidently, as Roger now had the scent of the chase in his nostrils. Mom and Dad were invited to join in the investigation, but I still pleaded my total lack of knowledge concerning the frame's defect. This, unfortunately, was my default way of dealing with situations which may be of detriment to me – attempt, unconvincingly, to lie my way out of it!

Without resorting to a full-on courtroom dispute I was judged guilty by implication, and my brother pronounced the bike to be scrap as the frame had been irreparably weakened by the mystery collision. "Oh, bloody hell!" was my innermost thought.

But fate came to the rescue, and after a Council of War involving the other three members of my family it was decided that another (new) bike would be purchased from the bike shop run by the local star racing cyclist, Bob Mansell. So I became the proud, if not sheepish, owner of a second new bike.

I wish to this day that I had shown the courage to admit that I had been in an accident on my bike. After all, I hadn't murdered anyone, so it was a fairly futile exercise on my part.

But this anecdote has been recounted to illustrate the fact that I hadn't the first idea how a bike needed to look, let alone how the parts worked.

As I have said, what is the point of having a big brother who is a genius with a spanner in his hand and a pile of bike parts at his feet? And remember, he was only 16 or 17 when this incident occurred. He had inherited Dad's engineering skills, while my genes had stubbornly refused to welcome those skills into my psyche.

My cycling career, or to put it more accurately, the period when I ceased riding a bike ended when I was about 16, and I had studiously avoided even blowing up a tyre with a pump by then. If ever I had a puncture, I would simply walk the bike home from the site of the mishap and ask my brother to fix it for me. At this stage the lure of knowledge of bicycle maintenance seamlessly into knowing nothing about car maintenance either; and the latter appeared to have a greater future for the inertia (aka bone-idleness) which was an unfortunate but intrinsic part of my make-up.

Fast forward then to 2007 and the engagement of my backside to a bike saddle, a marriage made in heaven, so to speak! (It is hard to imagine my backside and a bike saddle ever entering into holy matrimony but go with it.)

As my cycling odyssey began in the sparsely-populated French countryside in deepest, rural Brittany, I encountered my first puncture there in the middle of well, absolutely nowhere.

There followed a time-consuming walk home, and then I had to consider my next step.

A quick scan of the internet revealed that there was a bike shop about 10 kilometres hence on the outskirts of a neighbouring small town. I duly presented myself and my injured bike, and enquired in some hastily-learned French if they could possibly mend my puncture for me. They could, they did and charged me a reasonable sum for the privilege.

"That was painless enough," I thought to myself, not realising the frequency or the cost of the number of punctures I was going to suffer in the future. As my cycling mileage increased the inner tubes giving up on me increased exponentially. I found myself almost writing into my monthly budget an amount for puncture repair and inner tube purchase.

Many was the wet and windy dark morning or evening which would see me trudging wearily to the cycle repair shop with my wounded steed. I hadn't even worked out that by the swift usage of the quick release lever (clue's in the title!) then I could drop the wheel out and at least reduce the weight of the equipment I was carting to the bike hospital by just carrying the wheel there!

Occasionally I would wait for the repair to be accomplished to save my own time, and I did start to take an interest in what the mechanic was actually doing.

I should say at this point that I didn't realise that I possessed clincher tyres as opposed to tubeless. That particular penny wasn't going to drop until I took up riding on the track on a bike using tubeless tyres. Clincher tyres require an inner tube to be inserted, whereas tubeless tyres; well, you can work that out, can't you?

Back to the genius, sorry, mechanic. He seemed to stick into the wheel rim a plastic thingy (excuse the technical terms) which seemed to resemble one of those metal can openers. With a bit of elbow grease the edge of the tyre would pop over the rim of the wheel, and then it all seemed to follow around the rest of the circumference of the wheel. This, yes, you have guessed, was a tyre lever!

Forgive me reader, for I assume you know what I am talking about at this juncture, but I was standing there observing all of this as a complete ignoramus.

Then, the punctured inner tube would be peeled out of the wheel and a new one inserted and fed under the edge of the tyre, which, in turn, would be re-clinched to the wheel rim. Then, a one-handed inflation of the new tube with a state-of-the-art track pump; and hey presto, job jobbed!

Now, me being perhaps not the sharpest tool in the kit, started to compute that if I could do this operation myself, then I might be able to save not only the labour charges of the cycle shop, but also time as well in the old puncture pantomime. So I had to investigate teaching myself how to do it.

I found that I had some tyre levers in the makeshift toolkit my brother had put together for me so, I set about trying to remove the edge of the tyre from the rim. Roger would have laughed his socks off had he watched this performance.

After what seemed like an hour and a half, but what was probably only an hour and a quarter, I managed to get the edge of the tyre to comply. Sticking in a second tyre lever, some more of the rest of my life was used up getting a little more tyre edge to pop out. Then, pausing only to shave and get my hair cut, the rest of the tyre did as I had requested.

Next, I fed the inner tube into the wheel under the clincher tyre. Again, easier said than done. But curiously, I had more than enough inner tube for the rim. Hold on a second, didn't the genius, sorry again! mechanic, partially inflate the tyre at this stage? Yes, he had; and that did the trick as the inner tube now fitted snugly on the rim. All I had to do now was to get the side of the tyre to re-clinch the wheel rim, and off I set. This now turned out to be the most difficult operation of the lot. I could seat nine-tenths of the tyre on the wheel rim, but the last bit always seemed to be too tight.

I have to be honest here, that on more than one occasion I took the wheel back to the cycle shop and asked them to do the last bit for me. It habitually took about five seconds, to my usual acute embarrassment! In my defence, and to my sheer and utter relief, I did get better at this task. Several years down the line, I have reached the stage where I replace all my punctured inner tubes and tyres. You will not have the first idea how satisfied that has made me feel, but it has.

I mentioned the quick release levers on the wheels which enable the wheels to drop out of the frame. The front wheel is a really easy operation to drop out and put back in again. But the back wheel!!!

The first problem for me was lifting the derailleur out of the way. Eventually I could do this, but not without covering myself, and most of my clothing, in grease from the chain. Once removed, I perform the inner tube replacement surgery, and then I have to replace the back wheel on to the frame.

Well, that was an insoluble problem for me. This task, which should take about 15 seconds for any normally-skilled human being, I managed to get down to an average time, during my first 12 months of doing it, a few minutes. I was just plain useless at it. The reason was that I just didn't understand what the moving parts of the derailleur actually do.

Again, I was in the area of once or twice sheepishly taking the bike to a cycle shop and asking them to put the back wheel on to the frame. Even watching them do it didn't seem to help, but in the year of Our Lord 2020 I can report that this is something else that is now no problem for me.

By now you should be getting the feeling that you are reading the ramblings of a remedial bicycle mechanic. Well, yes you are!

My lack of mechanical skills came to a head a few months after I had been delivering Bikeability to schools in Birmingham.

On rainy days when the weather prevented us from going outdoors with the trainees, we would use the time profitably by doing something called Fix-it. The major activity of those sessions was removing a wheel from the bike, taking the tyre from off the wheel, removing the inner tube, mending a puncture, and then putting it all back together again to make the bike roadworthy once more.

I need to own up and say that even to this day, I have never successfully mended a hole in an inner tube, so I always put a new tube in to replace the punctured one! Mending the hole just continues to defeat me. I therefore had to do something about my absence of expertise, otherwise I was going to be shown up in no uncertain terms in front of my trainees for my total lack of skill and knowledge.

With a colleague of mine from Bikeability in Birmingham, I therefore enrolled for a two-hour basic mechanics course at a bike shop, and we duly underwent the syllabus. My problem was that we were split into pairs, and when the practical bits came up, I let my colleague do most of the repair work, and I didn't get as much out of it as I should have done.

I particularly wanted to see how to index gears, and we did go through that process; or rather my colleague did it, and to this day I still don't know how to do it. I could do with having that skill today, as I write this chapter. All of this was not my colleague's fault but my own, for not being assertive enough.

I don't know how to break a chain and insert or remove a link, and I should do. Nor can I replace a brake or gear cable, and I should do. Although I have the right tool, I can't remove a bottom bracket. I can't true a wheel after one has developed a slight buckle.

The list of things I can't do isn't endless, but would certainly fill the back of an average sized roll of wallpaper. I can, however, change pedals, although that took some heartache until I became even slightly proficient.

And I always remove and fit new brake blocks to my bikes, although I have frequently been told that I have put the blocks on back to front! I still work on the basis that if the bike stops when I ask it to, then my repair has been a success!

Unbelievably, I can now remove the gear cassette from a rear wheel and swap it for a different-sized one. All through purchasing the correct tool and looking at a cycle maintenance video on You Tube. One of my better achievements, that!

When I took up competing on the track, I had a bike that was about as basic as you could get, which almost suited me down to the ground! A track bike has no brakes, it has a single gear ridden on a fixed wheel. If one is competing in a multi-disciplined event on the track then it makes sense to change the sprockets, or cogs, to provide that different gearing ratio.

I learnt how to do that, under my brother's watchful eye. I was also able to fit my detachable tri-bars to the handlebars for events which allowed them. I suppose, when I was doing these things trackside, I looked as though I had a certain depth of knowledge; which I did, but the word "depth" is being used slightly out of context!

On any Monday morning when the Bikeability team goes into a school to start a new course, then we have to inspect each of the bikes for roadworthiness. This involves checking the tyres, the brakes for efficiency, and the chain, to ensure that it functions properly and keeps the bike moving as it should. But this A-B-C (Air-Brakes-Chain) leads to an unbelievable catalogue of problems with the trainees' bikes.

We get brakes that don't brake, so I have had to learn to adjust them so they work properly; pump up tyres with a track pump, which is almost certainly the only upper-body exercise I get; and free the chain when, for example, it has uncooperatively slipped off the cog and wedged itself against the bike's frame.

All of which makes me look like Dr Bike, the name we give to "on the hoof" maintenance sessions in schools, but it is basically me busking it. I now know enough to keep my own bikes on the road in a reasonably ridable state, but anything complex still has to go to the cycle repair shop.

For instance, I have recently purchased two bigger chain rings for my Time Trial bike, and that involves removing the pedals and putting on a new chain (I think!).   And that, at the moment, is beyond my skills.

I once asked the owner of a bike repair shop that I use frequently, as he is an ex-racer and fully understands what I need, how to perform a certain piece of bike maintenance. I was shot down in flames when he replied that if he told me how to do it, he would soon be out of business! Oh, OK. Please don't get me wrong, I really enjoy fettling and messing around with a bike, because when one has accomplished what one set out to do then there is a wonderful sense of achievement to be had.

I am getting better all the time. A couple of years ago I obtained a rusty old 1936 BSA tandem which I purchased for £25, and I spent a couple of months in my garage stripping it down to the frame. I learnt an awful lot doing that, and the only thing that defeated me was removing the bottom bracket. That whole experience was so enjoyable.

The project was to rebuild the tandem from scratch and after I had the frame resprayed in pillar box red by a local firm, and incidentally it looked fabulous, I sourced a lot of the new parts for it, and together with one or two salvaged pieces from the original machine, gave it to a friend of mine to assemble and make roadworthy.

Which of course he did; and it looked beautiful, and what's more, it worked. I sold it to a couple who live near Fort William in the Highlands of Scotland, and I had to remove most of the removable parts again in order to pack it up into a cardboard packing case for onward transhipment. All in all, a rewarding experience and I even made about £100 profit for my time and trouble!

To conclude this outpouring of honesty, which has probably confirmed my brother's observation of me all those years ago, all I can state in my defence is that I am improving all the time, and I am getting there.

By the time I am 100 years old I should be good enough to get a job as a mechanic with a professional racing team.

I can't wait!

CHAPTER FOUR

I Become a Time Triallist

Of course, with my sporting background, and as a keen follower of the sport of cycling, I knew what I had to do to become a participant; and that was to enter a Time Trial. In France these races are known as contre-le-montre: literal translation - against the clock.

This discipline of the sport was spawned between the two World Wars, when cyclists would meet in clandestine locations at the first light of day to race. By so doing they would hope to stay one step ahead of the police, who had outlawed such proceedings on the public highway. These days, every Time Trial takes place with prior sanction from the boys in blue.

The secrecy of these races meant that the meeting places and the courses themselves had to be disguised, because even in the days before the internet and other forms of social media, a clearly-stated venue would mean the police could step in and prevent the race. Therefore a code was introduced for the race courses; and to this day that code still pertains.

The body which administers time trialling in the UK is Cycling Time Trials (CTT). Their practice is to divide the country into regions alphabetically, and give each region an identifying letter. For example, first on the list is the Central region, and that is designated by the letter A. London South is G, and South Wales is R, to exemplify two more regions.

Next comes the distance to be raced, so a 10-miler is quite simply '10', or a '25' is a, well, you know. Then the courses themselves within each region are given a code number, so that everyone knows which course to turn up at.

So the G10/42 is a 10-miler in the London South region on course no 42 within that area. I think it is a super system.

Historically, time triallers were known by road racers as 'testers'. This they saw as a derogatory name, because they believed their road racing branch of the sport to be superior. To counter this slur, Time Trials are known the world over as "The Race of Truth", because once you have started your race then there is no hiding place. Quite simply, it is eyeballs out from start to finish, otherwise your time and performance suffers and you haven't been true to yourself.

Trawling the internet, I soon found that the month of December was out of the racing season. But I did find one race scheduled for the 30th of December put on by a cycling club called the Ogmore Valley Wheelers. The club secretary's phone number was there before my eyes, so I rang it and asked to enter the race, which was to take place on the R10/22. This was 'R' for South Wales, '10' for the distance and '22' to denote the actual venue and course for the race.

This was where my racing cycling education was about to begin in earnest. He explained that to participate in an official race (known as an 'Open' race, because it is open to any eligible rider) one had to be a member of a bona fide cycling club affiliated to the governing body the CTT. Otherwise, a rider wouldn't be covered by insurance during the race. I said that I wasn't a member of a club, and he said "Well, why not join ours?" So I did.

Ogmore Valley Wheelers, or the Oggies as they are known are based in Bridgend, a town about 20 miles or so west of Cardiff. The capital city of Wales itself has two thriving clubs, but as the Oggies claimed my valuable signature first, then I was lost to both Cardiff Ajax CC and its breakaway club (breakaway in the sense of a political schism, or row between its members) Cardiff Jif CC.

They chose their name with a sense of humorous irony, to keep the use of household detergents flying high in the valleys for names of cycling clubs. You have to laugh at their cheek!

I was now entered into the race and nerves began to jangle as the big day drew ever closer. Christmas had to be negotiated with all its excesses, but I kept riding on a daily basis throughout the festivities to maintain whatever level of fitness I had attained.

The time trial itself was a 10-mile race along the Glyn Neath road somewhere between the towns of Neath and Swansea. I was going to prepare for this race like a pro, and I hit on the idea of riding the full course the day before the time trial proper. Accordingly, I drove to the start point and unloaded the bike from the back of my car.

The weather was quite nice for South Wales in December I suppose – a howling gale, dark, glowering skies and sheets of torrential rain. I was clad in enough layers to have scaled Mount Everest without fear of frostbite, as I levered myself onto my aluminium steed, which was still my son's road, or racing bike. I laboured intensely riding the actual course the five miles out to the turn, and then set off for home directly into the teeth of said howling gale and got back to the car, tired, wet, dishevelled and wondering what the hell I had let myself in for. The following morning would hold all the answers to that particular question!

The day of the 30th of December 2007 dawned bright, sunny and clear, (he lied). It was even colder, even danker and yes, even wetter than the day before when I had bravely done my recce ride. The other time triallists were already there, fettling their racing machines, which were mostly full carbon bikes, with tribars fixed to their handlebars to draw the rider into the requisite aerodynamic position. And they were dressed head to foot in multi-coloured Lycra kit sporting the strips of their relative clubs.

Me? I turned up in about seven layers of warm lined clothing to combat the weather, and a woollen balaclava to keep my head warm underneath my standard road helmet, which was nothing like the pointed aero helmets being worn by these super athletes ranged before me.

I signed on to the start sheet, and was duly given my race number which was to be attached to my outer top garment by four safety pins. Having accomplished this, I rode the 3 or 400 yards to the start, where I joined the queue of riders lining up in number order to be sent on their way at one-minute intervals.

Of course, I had neglected to warm up, and I did notice that the other riders were sweating slightly, ready to go and dressed only in their skinsuits, in contrast to me wearing several kilograms of clothes. It was at this point that I wished I had never climbed on a bike in my whole life, as my nerves rendered me almost incapable of movement. But my turn arrived, and with the starter's fingers disappearing in front of my eyes to the count of 5 – 4 – 3 – 2 – 1, I was away.

Obviously, in order to make me the hero of this book, I should now report that that I gobbled up the course and spat it out, recording a time that everyone was astonished to see. Not a bit of it!

I set off into the wind and rain, and reached the halfway point in about 17 minutes. Circumnavigating the roundabout in order to re-join the dual carriageway, I was comforted and encouraged by the fact that the wind direction would now blow me home and take lumps out of my first half time. Not a bit of it!

The wind chose to traverse the island with me, and with a definite sense of cruelty, proceeded to blow into my face all the way to the finish, (or so it seemed to me) which I reached in about 34 minutes. The rest of the riders were on their second cups of tea; and what's more, they had scoffed all the biscuits when I turned up looking like I was in fancy dress, and as if I had done the time trial dressed as Wurzel Gummidge.

The winner of the race was some suntanned (remember the date!) lean Adonis from the Army (or might have been the Navy), who rode in bare legs, which were covered in some slick, shiny liquid to keep out the elements.

And I heard his girlfriend say to him that all that training climbing the Bwlch had paid dividends for him (the Bwlch being one of the steepest and longest mountain climbs in South Wales). That placed my soggy reconnoitre of a ride the day before into perspective.

But at least I had done my first-ever time trial, and whichever way you choose to interpret the preceding facts, I was now a racing cyclist, even if I was the worst one ever. Although, believe this or believe it not, I was to discover one or two who were not even as good as me in the days and months to come, he says, hallucinating!

Two obvious points that emerged from that first Time Trial were that I wanted to do more of them, and that I needed a proper time trial bike. I scoured the internet for a suitable second-hand machine to get me started properly, and eventually found one in my price range, being sold by a time triallist who lived in Coventry, some 130 miles away.

A brand-new bike was out of the question, as the costs would be prohibitive. And I was new to the discipline, so couldn't justify the cost, even though the machine would always have a resale value. I duly met the guy on a pub car park at Meriden, the geographical centre of England. That spot is actually marked by the National Cyclists' Memorial, to all the cyclists killed in the First World War. How appropriate could it get?

The vendor was a member of either the Coventry Cycling Club or the Coventry Road Club, I can't recall which; and he told me this machine had done a 24- minute 10-mile time trial. I thought, brilliant; but isn't it the guy riding it who gets the credit, because I was capable of riding a 34- minute 10 on any machine!

It was a Trek Time Trial frame, in silver, properly aero-dynamic with tri bars as part of the deal. It looked lovely, so I parted company with £750 and it was mine! This was to be the machine on which I was to ride my next 200 or so races, as I determined that I would get to grips with time trialling and become as good as I could be at it.

It was once put to me that when you take up time trialling your times will continue to improve for the first five years, and then you will plateau, i.e. you will find it difficult to record Personal Bests. I was no exception to this rule, and by mid-2010, in my third season of racing, I was frequently lowering my best times at the variety of distances at which I was competing. I used to find that I would start the season in February or early March in need of a gallop, to use horse racing parlance, or short of match fitness, to use football terminology. Anyway, you get the picture.

Then, as the races came along more frequently with the advent of the better weather and the longer days, my times would improve, and fitness-wise I seemed to be peaking annually around the start of June. The rest of the season, and there was always a long way to go from June to the end of the season with its multiplicity of races, I used to frustrate myself by having already recorded my best times for that particular season. This led to my inner resolve that I would make myself be able to race every single day of the year; in other words, maintain match, or race fitness constantly.

My Personal Best for 10 miles was set in 2010 on the K33/10 course near Alcester in Warwickshire one beautiful June Saturday afternoon. I was in my fourth season of racing, and even though I was now 59 years old, my times at most distances were improving all the time. Relying on the aforementioned mantra that, when you take up time trialling from scratch, you will continue to improve for five years and then you will plateau, I was certainly proving that theory to be correct.

The K33/10 is a mildly undulating course with some helter-skelter stretches which, if the conditions, i.e. wind direction, temperature, and humidity are stacked in your favour, then hopefully you are in PB territory. On this particular day it all came together, and I belted around the course at what was for me lightning speed, and took the chequered flag in 23 minutes 12 seconds; a time I have threatened on a few occasions since but never bettered.

It still remains an ambition of mine to improve that time and get into the 22s, but anno domini is conspiring against me as I am now 10 years down the line. But it remains a project.

One ambition which I did achieve, however, and that was to ride a sub-one hour 25. There is a course, again down at Glyn Neath in South Wales, the R25/3, which is probably the fastest course at that distance in the land. Everyone comes from far and wide to ride it and go home hopefully with a PB. The course itself involves a fast start northwards which is slightly downhill, and then you swing south onto the A road which goes sharply downhill for at least three miles. It is this stretch which will make or break anyone's record attempt, and when it levels out, time can still be gained as the turn for home comes at 15 miles and not the halfway distance.

The problem is that there is more than nine miles to ride to the finish along the valley, which if the wind is in the wrong direction, i.e. northerly, then it becomes an incredibly tough crawl to the line. Many a prospective, on-target, PB has foundered on this stretch thanks to the unforgiving north wind.

In 2012 I turned up on this course, not for the first time, with fitness in my legs and lungs; and if the conditions were favourable, high hopes in my heart. All seemed set fair as there was a light westerly breeze, a cross wind on this north-south racetrack, and away I went. I reached the first turn going well and turned to shoot down the steep hill which I called the "ski slope".

Putting my head down, I slammed my bike into top gear, which, I think was a 135-inch gear, and started to turn those pedals as fast as my little stubby legs would take me. At speeds well in excess of 40 miles an hour I maintained a cadence and a rhythm which saw me blast through the 10-mile mark in 21 minutes! Compare that to my 10-mile PB!!

I reached the turn at 15 miles in about 33 minutes, meaning that if I could grovel the last 10 miles or so in under 27 minutes, then I was home and hosed.

But on this glorious day no such grovelling was required, as a steady cadence saw me take the flag in 58 minutes 58 seconds. I had beaten the hour by over a minute! What a feeling that was.

Again, I have tried many times since to ride that course in similar conditions but they have never recurred. It only goes to show that on those days, which are few and far between, you have to be ready to capitalise, because you can't know when there will be a repeat. Still, I will keep on trying.

To date, the fastest speed I have ever reached on a bike stands at 44.6 miles per hour, and that was achieved during one of the Tuesday night time trials staged by the Severn Road Club, on a course which has its circuit close to the Aust Service Station under the M5 near Bristol.

This course involves a downhill start, which scares the living daylights out of you, as one immediately hurtles downwards at an outrageously ridiculous speed, avoiding a set of bollards halfway down. These force you to slalom around them, while praying that there is no traffic coming up the hill towards you. I rode this course many times, and I think I may have eased back a little in latter attempts, as there is a tendency for the bike to become out of control and develop a frightening speed wobble if you are not careful. Scary.

CHAPTER FIVE

Training Regimes

As a young footballer who came within a whisker of earning a professional contract, no-one could ever have described me as an enthusiastic trainer. Perhaps this was because the military style PT exercises we used to be subjected to were, in the short term, exhausting; and subconsciously they may have detracted from the real reason I was there, which was to learn to be a technically better footballer. Put a ball at my feet and I could run and run. But physiologically I had a tendency to put on weight whenever periods of relative inactivity took over.

As an adult I started to learn more about myself and my body and, coupled with definite goals, I would train under my own supervision, and obtain very good results from these self-imposed training regimes.

I took up jogging when I let my football career drift to a halt as I was hitting the 30-year-old landmark. Pounding the streets was, in itself, not the most pleasant of experiences, but with my penchant for sporting statistics this was an activity that I could log, and indeed, analyse.

But in my own complex little thinking processes I needed a goal, a target, something for which to strive. I decided, therefore, as a 1984 New Year resolution, to train for and enter the Wolverhampton Marathon, which was but 11 weeks away. My success (or otherwise) is chronicled elsewhere in this book, but what I actually achieved in those weeks was beyond what a lot of people could comprehend about me; and I had to listen to endless piles of relentless negativity about my training regime. This pleased me enormously, because I love taking on a challenge and proving people wrong!

I am now, to all intents and purposes, a teetotaller. I do partake of a glass of red wine if I go out to dinner, preferably Chateau Neuf-du-Pape, as that velvety drink goes down a treat, but only ever one glass. Over the course of a year I may drink about 12 to 15 glasses of red wine and no more. On the infrequent occasions that I actually go to a public house, I will boringly drink pop, fruit juice, coffee, tea or green tea.

I have not smoked since 2nd of December 1987 at 9.20 pm. I had been to a cricket meeting on behalf of Barclays Bank in London, and before climbing onto the train at Euston Station I bought a pack of 10 Benson & Hedges cigarettes (other brands were available!).

Chillingly, only two hours later, as the train pulled into Birmingham New Street Station, I had lit the last of those 10 cigarettes and my immediate, shocked thoughts were that I was killing myself, just as smoking took Dad from us so early. And also I couldn't afford the financial outlay of it. I was simply burning money.

Therefore I trod that 10th cigarette stub into the station platform, and can truthfully state that I have never wanted a cigarette from that day to this. That is how I have evolved over the years with regard to alcohol and smoking; and I am comfortable in my own skin.

Curiously, give me a challenge and I seem to rise to it. A throwback I suppose; to my schooldays when if I was told I shouldn't do something I usually went right on ahead and did it, usually to my detriment. A challenge appeals to the rebellious streak inside me. When you achieve something in the sporting arena, then it fuels the desire within you to carry on working at it and push on to the next level. In other words, keep right on going, and strive for improvement, constantly.

A mere three days after my 'epic' marathon run, after the stiffness miraculously disappeared, I once again donned my running shoes and incredibly ran my fastest ever time for 10 miles.

This all came about because I knew my own body, had come to learn things about it; when to push it, when to rest it, and most importantly, how to recover properly, which is an art a lot of people don't understand.

My brother will tell you that I don't understand the meaning of rest and recovery, and to a certain extent he is correct. But it is the inner guilt I feel if I don't train on a daily basis that powers me ever forwards. I do, however, feel the immense benefit of a rest day even if mentally it chews me up!

Pounding the streets, usually in the hours of darkness because I had a 9-to-5 job to satisfy, as well as a young family who needed to be laid down for the night, meant that training had to be planned and purposeful. During the day one's mind moves to that night's training. What do you want to do, where do you want to do it, and what do you want to achieve? Do you want to do something better than the night before, or better than you have ever done it?

My constant training companion was always a stopwatch, and I knew the exact distances of everywhere I used to run. This became an exact science with me because this was before the days of computers and sat-navs, which measure and log everything for you these days.

Having a mind which could compute information very quickly by the use of mental arithmetic, I might get to the closing stages of a run and quickly calculate that I had, say five minutes to beat my best time on any particular training course.

So mentally you go for it, and your body lets you go for it because your fitness levels have increased to the point where you can up the tempo and then put in a sprint finish. There aren't many better feelings than finding you have the energy to do a sprint finish; and then the next night, the sprint finish might start earlier and ergo, last longer.

This type of outcome is rewarding as all the statistics tell you that you are making improvements all the time. This is what British Cycling famously call Marginal Gains.

Swimming is always a useful cross-training outlet. As an endurance athlete on the bike, and to a certain extent on the roads, I have found no problem with diving into a swimming pool, even after an absence from this discipline of several years, and swimming straight off a mile at breaststroke.

This activity alone for someone of my age and build can burn off 900 calories per hour and it is, of course valuable exercise for the upper body, this being an area which can become neglected by regular cyclists.

Curiously, I can ride in excess of 100 miles in one day without any fuss, but walking around a shopping centre is knackering. Or is that something to do with spending money, to which we all have an aversion, however latent!

On the subject of the upper body, the game of squash is, I believe a brilliant activity for improving and taking your fitness levels to heights you have not reached before. I have played squash for over 30 years so that time span has coincided with some periods when my weight has been shamefully out of control. But by the same token, when I have been in a spell of controlled and improving fitness, I have only to look at the shape and tone of my leg muscles as I walk in a pair of shorts to the squash court to see the effects of taking this game seriously.

Nowadays, I regrettably don't play squash at all because my playing partner Dave, who is eight years my senior, decided to hang up his racquet at the age of 70.Furthermore, the ravages of my sporting career have rendered both of my wrists way short of the strength required to play the game without pain.

Positive thinking should always accompany you in your training regime.

Always look for one or more positives out of any training spell you have undertaken. For example, if I completed a 10-mile run which was a PB and the next night I equalled that time exactly, then where is the marginal gain? Your mind should now be attuned to positivity and therefore the PB is that you are a day older and the second of the two runs is the more meritorious by virtue of your advancing age!

There is your marginal gain in the stats, and if anyone pooh-poohs that way of thinking, then it is none of their business and they probably aren't as advanced in their own thinking and comprehension of what is going on. How could they be, when it is your own body and performance level that you are analysing?

The foregoing theory may well be construed as a load of tosh, but it is, above all, also an exercise in positive thinking, and a healthy and co-operative mental process is a great boon to successful training. So, when the great day of the 1st of September 2007 arrived, and I re-acquainted myself with the bicycle, I had a personal wealth of training data locked inside me which I would bring strongly to the fore, even though on that date I was, quite simply, a tub of lard!

But I have to be totally honest, because when I did finally climb on the bike it was an exploratory exercise. I couldn't possibly have envisaged that it would so quickly become my life-changing experience, so there was no preconceived training plan in place. It was only as I developed a daily riding pattern and things started happening, such as weight loss, and improved fitness levels, that I started to bring forward theories and concepts which had worked for me as a runner.

First of all, I began to plan my daily rides, albeit subconsciously, as my thoughts turned quite normally to when my next ride would be, where and over what distance and time of day. As I mentioned earlier, marshalling your thoughts in this way is an early stage of getting into a meaningful and disciplined training regime.

Then, the next stage is to action it, and by that I mean don't let anything stand in your way.

For example, it is the easiest thing in the world to decide not to ride for a variety of reasons, such as the weather being too wet, or too cold or you are too tired or it is too late or you feel you are due a rest day. All of these are huge negatives and allowing one or more of these reasons to prevent you from riding is a backward step.

Discipline yourself to get out there and get it done, and then you will allow the endorphins, the feel-good sensations in your body, to grip you post-effort as you feel so, so good about yourself. I have long since been at the stage where I can't live with myself if I don't ride on a daily basis.

Keep your own records, and importantly keep them up to date. When you sit down with your post-ride hot drink and that wonderfully refreshing food that you have earned with your efforts, then do your stats. Log them, look at them and make projections in addition to looking back.

At the time of writing I currently have six bikes, all of which perform a different function for me. I log the mileage that I have ridden on each of these bikes, which provides data in a number of ways, not least when I come to replace a bike or an important moving part.

For example, if you have ridden 425 miles in 16 days in a 30-day month then you are on target to ride 797 miles that month. If that is below what you wanted to finish up with at month end, then up your mileage. If it is above your expectation, then work out an average daily figure to keep you above your target. Either way you are using your stats positively.

Log all sorts of data. I record miles done on a daily, monthly, year to date and career to date basis, and also the number of days ridden in succession. This can lead to all sorts of useful information which can be channelled into planning or just plainly sitting down and analysing your achievements thus far.

In one period leading up to February 2016 I actually rode for 908 days in succession, or two and a half years without a single day off.

What's more, I averaged in excess of 31 miles a day for that period. I wouldn't have known all that without my diaries being chock full of day-on-day information.

On one occasion I had to catch a flight from Luton Airport, which necessitated checking in at 5.30 am. Notwithstanding a two-hour road journey to reach the airport, I set the alarm clock for midnight, and promptly rode 10 miles on my rollers, so that by one in the morning I had kept my run of successive days training alive and kicking.

As a postscript, I used to set up my rollers in front of the TV set in my lounge on days of inclement weather, to ensure that I was still putting in a useful training session. And this was what happened to end that run of 908 successive days' training.

Riding on the rollers in front of the telly presented problems, because if, for example, I was watching a footie match on the box, then when a player slung over a cross and the camera followed the trajectory of the ball, then my eyes would follow it and I would become disorientated on the rollers. Anyone who has ridden on this specific training aid will know that one has to concentrate to keep balanced, as if you shut your eyes you would soon be on the floor.

To give me a safety net I used to turn the coffee table onto its side on my right hand at waist level, to give me something to grip on that side if I felt I was about to ride off the rollers and I had the welcoming softness of the settee to dive onto if I came off on my left side.

Problem was, on this specific day I had unknowingly positioned the rollers forward of their usual siting, so that I was level with the settee arm and not the soft cushions.

When the inevitable happened and I lost my balance, I threw myself towards the awaiting cushions expecting the pre-planned soft landing, only to hit the upholstered arm, which contained a solid block of wood, as all furniture builders will know!

My ribs hit the wood of the arm hard, and I came down in a real tangle. Suddenly, I was engulfed in the most excruciating pain, and all the air was evacuated from my lungs. I picked myself up as best I could, and then realised that I was winded, and my next breath was not materialising. I was gasping for breath and nothing was happening, I squatted down on the floor as the pain was now kicking in big time and I just couldn't breathe. Eventually after what seemed an eternity but was in reality at least a couple of minutes I started to get control of my lung functions again but I was in extreme agony.

My ribs were severely damaged, and the pain was now taking over. Foolishly, I didn't go to hospital that night and had to sleep in an armchair because it was impossible for me to lie down as the pain would not allow it. I spent five nights in that armchair during which time I had it confirmed that I had broken a couple of ribs but on the fourth day, misguidedly, I was back on the rollers. Albeit gingerly, because I reasoned that I was uninjured from the waist down so I needed to, literally, get back in the saddle.

This latter act of returning to the bike can be construed as sheer lunacy, but I was so worried that all my hard-earned fitness gains would be dissipated by this debilitating injury. It is said that you can interpret statistics any way you want, and I have always done just that. So I was not going to take the ending of my proud 908-day training streak in the best of humour without fighting back, now was I?

When one becomes a time triallist then I think it is a useful discipline to log all of your race information. I keep records, season by season of every aspect of every race. I have the date of the race, the course code, the distance, my time, the sequential number of that race, both by season and by career. Then when I need to know what my course best, or season's best, or even PB is then I can fish it out immediately.

These days I log the weather information, i.e. the wind speed and direction, and the overhead conditions including the temperature.

I then analyse my performances in the 10-mile time trials, as this is the distance over which I compete three quarters of the time. I can see at a glance in which minute the bulk of times are following, and this takes the form of a numerical graph. So, if I am knocking in a good proportion of times in the 25-minute bracket, then I can compare that to my season's average time, and indeed my career average time. I am firmly of the belief that it is better to have this information to hand and use it, than to ride willy-nilly without the first idea of whether you are in a run of good form or are getting back to form, after say injury or illness.

I have every one of my 552 races logged in this way, and if it is the last thing I look at when I hang up my cycling shoes, then I will know what I have achieved. Call it anally-retentive if you want to, but I am not alone in doing this, as I have frequently heard riders saying that today they are reaching a landmark, for example their one thousandth race. I was speaking to a guy recently who said he was approaching his 1,250[th] time trial, a real landmark. I asked him how he would feel when he had achieved it, and he replied with an impish grin across his face "Tired!". Can't argue with that!

So that is how I train using numbers and the written word. I would like to share with you now how I physically train, but please bear in mind that I am not a world champion, or indeed any sort of champion (although I was the 60 to 64 Veteran Time Trial Champion of Wales in 2009, I think it was). Please refer to the chapter 'When I became a Time Triallist' for the full Pathe News-style report of that monumental victory!

Chris Boardman stated that if you race on a Time Trial bike then you should train on your Time Trial bike. That is what I try to do from time to time, as this gives you a good feel of where you are, fitness-wise in between races.

You can either ride at, say 90%, of your race pace and keep your fitness levels topped up, or go for a full-on race effort with a timed ride over a known course.

On a day-to-day basis I use my road bike, as my job teaching Bikeability in schools means that I have a ready-made training ride which I can usefully utilise, to get to and from work, always with a fully loaded rucksack on my back. Sometimes I push myself on these rides, and sometimes I use them sensibly as a recovery ride. All of this mileage I log in my diaries, and after all these years I now have an astonishing amount of data from which I can draw and interpret any way I wish.

I have this mantra that I want to keep myself race-fit 365 days of the year. In other words, I can get myself out and ride a time trial without a moment's notice on any given day. I have been at that personal level for some time, (injuries excepted during 2017-18). It is the outcome of my 12-and-a-half years of continuous riding, and although I am not a champion by any definition of the word, in my own mind I have gone far beyond what I imagined I could achieve.

There is in fact no limit to what is possible. My regime, which is to ride every day, has got me where I want to be. It will not be to everyone's suitability to do exactly as I do, but for a 22-and-a-half stone ageing chap like me, then boy, has it worked!

And why not ride every day? First of all, I derive the most enormous pleasure from it, it has got my weight down (9-and-a-half stones shed), my health has improved, at the very least I haven't had a headache for 12 years – honestly – and my clothes fit me. Take simple things like walking up a flight (or more) of stairs: this I can accomplish without even breathing slightly heavily. My stamina has improved beyond all recognition, and I have even been out jogging for a mile or two on, admittedly infrequently, a number of occasions. This I think is beneficial, as it exercises other parts of the body which cycling perhaps doesn't.

Riding every day, and there will now follow a statistic which I am not able to substantiate but which I firmly believe, puts me in the top 99.99% for fitness in the whole of the UK for my age group.

I don't know how many 69-year-old men there are in this country, but I am willing to bet that there will be no more than one in ten thousand of them who are fitter than me, or who currently knocks in the numbers I do. It can't be proved, but at the same time I can't be far off with that boast, now can I?

Treat every ride on the bike as a training ride, no matter how short. Extract the positives from them and look at your marginal gains. But, never lose sight of the fact that riding a bicycle is one of the most pleasurable activities available to you.

I currently possess six bikes and every one of them does a different job for me. First of all is my flying machine, my time trial bike, which is the third aero-dynamic steed I have owned. This is a Boardman, which while not the highest spec, nevertheless does the job for me and within my budget.

Then I have two road bikes, one being a full carbon Pinarello FP2 which I bought for £900 in the summer of 2019 after its octogenarian racing cyclist owner decided his racing days were over. This bike, I like to think, is worth considerably more than what I paid for it, and I can state categorically that this is the best road bike I have ever ridden, it is an absolute joy.

The second road bike is a bog-standard Decathlon Triban 500 road bike which doubles as my work bike and occasionally my training bike. I have another Triban 500 road bike which I am about to strip but which could easily be resurrected and made roadworthy again. It is this latter bike on which I conquered Alpe d'Huez Decathlon so can feel free to use that as a testimonial for these machines!

My fifth bike is a folding bike made in the USA provided by my employer and which acts as a back-up for work on days where the weather is lousy or when I can't get meaningfully out on the road.

My sixth and final bike is my track bike, a V-Sprint frame with V-Sprint wheels and this of course will propel me around the velodrome on any future assaults on the World Championships.

You don't have to have only one bike, but if you do, look after it and it will look after you. Your body holds to the same principles in that if you look after what the Good Lord has given you then it will more than look after you. Your body will actually reward you with better and better performances. The more you scientifically push your body then the better it will perform.

But what I am really banging on about is about the knowledge that you build up about yourself is yours to retain and help with the improvements and maintenance of condition you are seeking in your desire to be a competitive cyclist, even at my amateur level.

Everything is relative. I know how far to push myself and what I need to do to improve. For example, if I want to make my sprinting performances better then I devise a series of training blocs where the effort I put in is actually a fraction harder than if I was involved in race conditions.

I may, for example, want to become quicker over 200 metres, so I will devise a series of reps - repetitions – over anything from 300 to 500 metres, or even replicate the actual distance of 200 metres but do it up a slight incline, so that when I need a 200 metre burst, either indoors or outside then I have already done something harder and I can quickly perform at 100% maximum.

And then my 100% max might then get better, so that my top performance improves pro rata. It may not be as scientific as the pro boys do at British Cycling, or within the strict training regimes of Team INEOS, but it works for me. And I am sure someone working with me who has similar goals would benefit from the way I do things. It is all a far cry from when I first climbed on the bike in 2007 carrying vast quantities of excess physical baggage. But it is a truism that you live and learn, and I am still learning.

My hill-climbing ability, which as recently as three years ago was non-existent, owes its massive improvement to the day I told myself that the best way to get better at climbing hills is to climb hills.

This does work, and I have already done over 500 designated ascents in training. It is also one of the maxims I regularly trot out to the long-suffering trainees on my Bikeability sessions; but there it is harder to get the message across as, not being regular cyclists like me, then climbing to them is anathema and to be avoided at all costs!

When the weather is bad, and remember it rains an awful lot in the UK and there is plenty of ice, frost and snow to boot, then I continue cycling and ergo training indoors. I either use my rollers, which are a godsend to me, or I use my local gym membership and ride the static bike.

I have done a tremendous amount of work on these machines, which record your elapsed time, your speed and your cadence (your pedalling frequency). As a training aid I have found them invaluable and I have done dozens of 40-mile rides on these machines measuring myself against my PB every time I climb on. I believe my record was 1 hour 43 minutes which isn't too shabby for that 40-mile effort.

My method is simply to keep pedalling, sweating buckets in the process, and very often looking out of the window as the ravages of the English weather remind me why I am on this contraption in the first place. I actually love the static bike, and recommend its use to any competitive cyclist as a change of "scenery" to freshen up the daily training regime.

I have also kept a daily food diary for the last 12 years. After I had been cycling for about six months, I decided that it was time to up the ante if I wanted to make my way as a time triallist, and above all, be as competitive as I could be in that particular discipline, so I booked an appointment with a nutritionist.

I was professionally informed what was good to eat and drink, and what was not; which foods would provide me with energy; and how and when to consume my dietary intake. The best piece of advice that I was given was to keep a daily food diary, recording the calorific content of everything I ate and drank, and then netting off the calories I burnt through exercise. This would then calculate for me my net daily calorie intake. If applied to the rule that an adult male needs 2,500 calories per day to maintain their weight, then any figure below that benchmark should lead to a loss in weight.

So in February 2008 I started my food diary, and I have kept it going religiously from that day to this. And you know what? It works. I know the calorific value of everything I consume and my cycle computers tell me how much energy I have burnt off during each effort. Importantly, don't cheat yourself with your recordings. You will be the loser if you artificially manipulate your readings, so be honest at all times.

I also keep a daily average calorie consumption figure throughout the month to see whether I am doing better or worse than the previous month or months and I weigh myself as soon as I get out of bed every single day, with the scales in the same spot in the bathroom so I can properly compare like with like.

All of this data is, of course, recorded in my diaries and is available to me as I analyse where I am at and how to progress, and the effects of unusual activity such as the Christmas and New Year periods, with their natural excesses, holiday times or even going to a restaurant for a meal are there in black and white for me to consider. There is never any need to despair when you have a sudden weight gain, and this should not be used negatively as an excuse to trigger a spell of inertia and a fall back from your training routine. Simply use it as a catalyst to work a little harder in the short term to blow away any extra pounds and you will be back where you were, or where you want, or expect to be.

The other little tool that I use and log statistics from is a blood pressure monitor. After my weight had ballooned to its highest level when I was in my mid-fifties my GP prescribed for me two tablets to lower my soaring blood pressure and a third to control my cholesterol.

The combination of these pills and my cycling regime meant that my blood pressure lowered dramatically and; as I have stated elsewhere in this book a nurse at the Queen Elizabeth Hospital in Birmingham said that I had, despite being in my sixties, the equivalent resting heart rate of a 21-year-old serving soldier, and she asked how I did it.

You should know what my one-word answer to that query was. Yes, it was "Cycling!"

Much to my chagrin the GP won't take me off these tablets even though I cycle considerable distances on a daily basis. I hope I never fail a random drugs test after a race although I do have the official medical prescription authorising the use of these tablets! I take my blood pressure every day when I first leap out of the sack and every night last thing before I turn in, so I am always comparing like with like and of course I log the readings assiduously.

I had a cold recently which I couldn't shake off for ages, and it is interesting and informative to see how one's blood pressure and resting heart rate react to one's detriment during these down times and you can also see when your body is on the road to recovery. Information overload? Not a bit of it, simply knowing your body and using the data provided to get yourself back on an even keel.

Before a race I have a strict routine, which I believe prepares me for the upcoming test. First of all, I have a drink of black filter coffee, to give me the caffeine boost I am seeking. I can't abide instant coffee which to me is tantamount to imbibing coloured dust. The caffeine, *au naturellement,* will have a detrimental effect on my bladder, but that is factored into the equation.

Then I will spray my leg muscles with a heat spray (I am resisting the temptation here to advertise for once), whether the weather be warm or cool, as it makes my legs feel warmed up. It can save me a layer of clothing, and therefore weight on the bike during the race, as it acts as tantamount to spraying on a pair of leggings and insulating my legs. Remember, weight loss is free speed on the bike. It all adds up, marginal gains and positive thinking once more.

Then I will have a couple of caffeine tablets, as we are getting into stimulant overdose now, followed by half a packet of glucose tablets, which weigh in at 87 calories, and then top off this veritable feast with an energy gel, those little sachets which were once unforgettably described to me as fruit flavoured snot!

I then climb onto my time trial bike and ride to the start hoping to cover anything up to 10 miles, which I ride at touring pace, husbanding my resources at the correct time, i.e. before the race starts. When I reach the line, I know mentally I have prepared exactly how I wanted to, and I am by dint of all that, physically ready to go.

Oh, and mustn't forget a dive into the bushes to relieve Monsieur Bladder, who by now is screaming at the top of his voice. (Do bladders have a voice? Discuss. Or rather – don't!)

Other people do things differently, some may pound away on their rollers or turbo trainers at the side of their cars (selfishly robbing the car park of parking space, but I digress), and work up a real sweat, but I have never done that. The top boys usually prepare this way. (Note to self, try it sometime).

It may all sound like information overload, and if it is, then so what? I have at my fingertips all the information I need to know about my most important possession, my body. We all train in different ways, I have set out what I do, and how it works for me. Am I obsessive? Perhaps. But again, so what? I treat myself as a 69-year-old professional cyclist, and if I can't actually live the dream because I am too old to sign a professional contract, notwithstanding a vast shortfall in the requisite talent, then, you know what? I can still live my own personal dream, which only involves me and the bike, of course.

In 2014 I enrolled for an Elite Personal Trainer course which would give me a qualification to be an actual Personal Trainer in a gym. This course was over a six-week period starting in November, and after four weeks would break for Christmas and resume for the final two weeks in the New Year.

Now this course did not come cheap, so a considerable outlay meant that I had to knuckle down and get myself qualified, which I did. It was an immensely enjoyable course and naturally I was the oldest participant by some considerable distance.

There were younger men and women from various walks of life who all brought different skillsets and backgrounds to the table, but we all mucked in and were a good supporting band of brothers (and sisters). The course content covered subjects such as the physiology of the body, and how muscles and tendons and other bits and bobs worked; and there was a large content on dietary and nutritional requirements.

There was huge emphasis placed on physical demonstrations of our newly learnt knowledge, because you can't be a Personal Trainer sitting in an armchair, you actually have to get out there and demonstrate what you expect your clients to perform. This was not easy for me as my fitness levels, at the age of 64, had to be good enough to enable me to perform all of these physical activities in the correct manner; and I surprised myself by doing so to an acceptable level.

Then one had to devise written training programmes for "clients" and then demonstrate these and put them into practice. Again, not easy. All of these demos were marked by examiners, and if you didn't meet the desired level then you were going to fail the course. Coupled with all of that there were several written papers of the multiple-choice answer variety. If one didn't meet the pass mark first time around you were given the opportunity of a resit within a couple of days, but with, I think, a slightly higher pass mark required.

I managed to get through all of the written exam papers first time except one, which was on the physiology subject matter of the syllabus, but with some last-minute cramming, I succeeded.

So, at the end of six gruelling but highly enjoyable weeks, I was a qualified Elite Personal trainer. Now came the hard part, getting myself taken on by a gym. I went to most of the big gym chains and they were all pleased to have me on board, but only after I had contracted to pay them their weekly rental for use of their gym facilities.

Also, I was going to have to find my own clients. The engagement would be on a self-employed basis, and the only certainty was that I had to pay the gym the weekly rental.

In the end I agreed to work at Fitness First in Solihull, near Birmingham, which was situated a 10-mile bike ride cross city from my home. I began working for the gym in February 2015. This all began to look like slave labour, as I had to give several unpaid hours a week to the gym's general dogsbody rota whilst attempting to pick up a client bank at the same time. This meant being at the gym for its 6 a.m. opening time some days, or clearing up at its 11 p.m. closing time on others. These would then be either preceded or followed by the cycle ride to or from home, in whatever weather and in total darkness. Bearing in mind I was in my 65th year I wondered what, stupidly, I had let myself in for.

Clearing up the gym at night so that it could reopen the next morning in a tidy and usable condition was a real chore, because the members in the weights room were collectively a bunch of idle (and muscular) buggers, leaving us instructors to put the weights not only away, but away in their correct weight order in the racking, some of which was at a height that meant I was getting a better workout than they were!

This was a tough assignment for me, and one night I dropped a 20-kilogram barbell directly onto my big toe, which immediately caused all the wax to be expelled from my ears as well as an intense pain. Fortunately, nothing was broken, except for my resolve. I needed clients quickly to make this thing pay or I would be sunk.

What I had envisaged in order to make me stand out and offer something that no-one else offered was to give spinning lessons in the cycling studio on a regular basis. This didn't materialise, because the existing spinning classes all seemed to consist of an instructor yelling out instructions in a pseudo-American accent whilst accompanied by a boom-bang-a-bang musical track, whereas I wanted to dispense with the music altogether, and run sessions for competitive cyclists who would top up or improve their fitness levels. Didn't happen.

I did though, have a couple of successes. One was with a lady who had seen at least 50 summers. She had signed up for a charity ride from Vietnam to Cambodia, and her cycling experience was restricted to riding to the supermarket and back. But I turned her into a wonderfully fit endurance cyclist, who had the time of her life on her adventurous ride by taking her out on longer and longer rides around the Warwickshire country side, putting into practice many of the techniques I had taught myself on my own personal cycling odyssey, and not those culled from my Elite Personal Trainer course.

The other was with a teenage couple who were competitive Latin American ballroom dancers, with their eyes targeted firmly on the World Amateur Championships. They came to me to improve their strength and conditioning, as they were already as fit as fiddles. Their opinion of the professional dancers on Strictly Come Dancing was unprintable, as they believed they had sold their souls to the devil and turned away from the true ethos of their sport!

I had some very enjoyable sessions with them until sadly, I had to pull the plug on the whole gym training experience because I wasn't making any money, and also my instructing in Bikeability was taking up more and more of my time, and more profitably.

Having been a competing sportsman already for over 60 years I am, like countless others of my ilk, extremely superstitious. I mention it in this chapter on training because now I have become a competitive rider, I use these foibles as motivational techniques. Let me explain by going back first to previous sports in which these superstitions took hold.

As a footballer I always put on my right boot first, even though I am left-handed. It felt comfortable and natural, and eventually I believed I wouldn't have a good game if I donned the left shoe before the other. Some pro footballers always insist on being the last player onto the pitch, and Paul Ince always entered the playing area bare-chested and put his shirt on the moment his feet touched the green sward.

Cricket has multiple superstitions, and I signed up to most of them. If you were part of a team who were batting second in a game, that is, chasing down the opposition's score to win the game, then if you were one of the non-batters watching from the pavilion you never, ever changed your seat. If you did, you were invited to return to your original seat, in case luck dictated that the run chase would falter and be ultimately unsuccessful.

If the team score, or an individual's score reached 111, this is known as "Nelson", and in England it is the unlucky number. (Nelson had 1-1-1 – i.e. one eye, one arm, one heart, or that was his body inventory the day he died!) So again, if you were sitting in the pavilion as part of the batting side when the score reached Nelson, then you kept both feet off the ground until the score moved on. Sometimes when the score stagnated on this number it would murder your stomach muscles; but see the positive, and treat it as good training and core conditioning.

In Australia 87 is termed the "devil's number" as it is13 short of 100 (another unlucky number, due to the traitor Judas Iscariot being the 13th person at the Last Supper). Any multiples of Nelson, e.g. 222, 333 etc receive the same "feet off the ground" treatment.

The famous Test Match umpire, the late and much-lamented David Sheppard, himself a former professional player, used to hop from one foot to another when Nelson was on the scoreboard, as it is not possible to levitate with both feet off the ground when standing, as umpires have to!

As a batsman I always put on my left pad before the right. Also, if a new item of kit is purchased, then it should always be used for the first time in practice. It must never be used for the first time in a competitive match, as you are inviting a poor performance personally, or a team defeat.

I got myself into a real superstitious impasse when, at the end of every over while I was batting, I used to cross myself, (genuflect) and utter a silent prayer to our Maker that I would survive the next over.

That eventually manifested itself into me genuflecting before I received every delivery. Nobody ever noticed this or if they did never commented. They probably just thought it was an habitual scratching of an itch or a gentle wipe away of any sweat on my face.

I do however have a problem with players, particularly footballers, praying for victory or good performance in a sporting arena because your opponents may be praying to the same God; and there can't be two winners of a game. This never stopped me doing it though, selfishly and hypocritically.

Moving on to cycling, I still invoke the new kit thing, and as cycling seems to involve the constant purchase of such items, I ensure these items are pressed into service for the first time during training blocs.

But the big one with me, which I use several times during any one ride, is the "Nelson' superstition. I have a habit of counting my pedal strokes, my cadence, particularly when I am riding up a hill. If the hill is a well-known obstacle, then I know how many pedal strokes I need to put in before I crest the summit.

This is particularly relevant if I am standing up on the pedals. When counting, I will not say, albeit silently, 1 - 11, or 2 - 22 and so on.

I replace the offending number with 'la-de-da' which seems to fit the appropriate space perfectly. In this way I use the "Nelson" syndrome, if I can call it that, as a motivational technique, and indeed, as a very useful training tool. My thinking is that if I actually mistakenly say the number, even silently, then I have the belief that something awful will befall me, such as being certain to have a puncture in the next two minutes.

Therefore, if I say 1 - 11 instead of la-dee-da, then I have to ensure I keep counting to the next Nelson number, and so replace 2 - 22 with the appropriate la-de-da. First sign of insanity? Yeah, probably. But as always, it works for me, so give it a whirl and you might find that you develop your own motivational superstitions.

Am I an obsessive-compulsive disorder candidate? Perhaps I am, when it comes to cycling. But the fitness levels I have reached both mentally and physically mean that I am in control of my own destiny, with all my OCD-gathered info to hand to help me understand my most important possession – me.

I don't know if any of this training malarkey that I have outlined in the preceding paragraphs would work for you, reader, but if there is anything in this chapter which might help you, then please don't die wondering.

CHAPTER SIX

Testing Times

Time Trialling has been, and I hope will continue to be, the most fulfilling of pastimes for me. As a 'Tester', I have become extremely fit for my age, and regularly get the biggest kick out of pushing myself to my absolute limits. The effect it has had on me physiologically is astonishing.

I am healthier, slimmer and have, so I was told by a nurse in the Queen Elizabeth Hospital, Birmingham, where the wounded soldiers from the Middle Eastern conflicts are taken for treatment, the resting heart rate of a 21-one-year-old serving soldier. (And he's not having it back!)

From an unfit, unhealthy 22-and-a-half stone heart attack in waiting I have become as fit as I have ever been in my life, and I am now in my 70th year. It has been a wonderful experience so far, and as an ex-clubmate of mine in the Oggies once yelled to anyone within earshot, he intends to be riding competitive time trials when he is 95. So, never one to shirk a challenge, I am aiming to go to at least the age of 96. And why not? The spirit and the flesh are both willing, and some!

I witnessed a time trialling legend in the flesh last year when I rode a race in Nottinghamshire. I pulled into the car park and parked alongside 83-year-old Ron Hallam, a guy I have raced against before, and someone who I believe has been a champion in the past, as well as an age-group winner nowadays. He was putting in a pre-race training bloc on his turbo trainer next to his car and really turning the pedals. His start time was still at least an hour away.

He then rode his race going off some minutes before me, meaning that when I returned to HQ after my race, Ron would be savouring his cup of tea and cake. Oh no he wasn't, he was back on his turbo trainer, warming down, and putting not just me, (and I was giving him 15 years) but every other competitor in the 100-strong field to shame. Now that really is what I call a time trialling legend. Chapeau Ron.

But time trialling has literally been testing at times, and my 552 races (at the time of writing) have now and again been fraught with difficulties and problems (and no little humour) along the way, so here are just a few of my (mis)adventures).

I first took the giant step up of entering a 25-mile time trial during 2008, in my first season of racing. Now armed with my Trek aero-dynamic speed machine, I figured I had the fitness and ability to cope with the greater distance, which was, of course, 2 and a half times further than I had raced before. Entering the race was the easy part, but as the event drew ever closer, I started to become really nervous as to what I had let myself in for, so at least a familiar pattern was developing!

The course was an out-and-back route along the A40 from a start somewhere outside Llandovery to Carmarthen and back. A lot of it would be raced on the dual carriageway but also, being Wales, it was certainly not going to be flat. As I queued at the start my nerves were really taking hold, but I had warmed up properly, eaten glucose tablets for energy and filled myself with black filter coffee to give me the boost, or rocket fuel that I needed. The weather was typical for a time trial in mid-Wales – windy with heavy rain. Oh joy!

When you are on the start line all sorts of daft thoughts surface to make you lose whatever mental reasoning you may still possess. Such as, just how do the meteorological gods know when there is a race on, so that they can summon up the requisite hideous weather?

Anyway, push literally came to shove on the start line and off I set.

This distance really was uncharted territory for me, but I satisfied myself by getting into a decent rhythm on the pedals, despite the downright awful weather.

Out in the open countryside after about eight or nine miles I suddenly experienced a familiar urge. I should point out at this juncture that my bladder is a bloody nuisance. It and I are frequently not on the best of terms, as it persists in drawing attention to itself at the most ridiculously inconvenient moments, and this just had to be one of them.

I was in the middle of a race and the bucketful of filter coffee I had downed before the race was now screaming for release. I searched for a convenient bush or tree behind which I could duck, and in this particular spot in the Principality that in itself was no problem, as only the sheep would be tut-tutting as I relieved myself; but, hang on bladder, I am in the middle of a race here. You don't see Bradley Wiggins parking his bike to dash into the Gents during the Tour de France, now do you? (I am not even going to mention Paula Radcliffe, as this is a family show!)

Therefore, like any elite athlete, I thought quickly, and weighed up the circumstances. It was raining heavily; I was wearing black; I was in the middle of nowhere, and there was no other living soul around. So I decided just to do it in my skinsuit on the bike whilst I continued pressing on with my racing duties. I accomplished that particular mission and the incessant rain washed me clean before my bike computer had clicked over many more miles. Me - 1, bladder - 0. This has not been a situation I have had to repeat too often thankfully, but it showed I was at least thinking like a proper racer. I had continued on my tortured way, to complete the race, relieved in more ways than one, and definitely more comfortable!

One of my early time trials in that first season was a short 3-mile uphill dash which was stage one of a three stage race for veterans. In the sport of cycling one reaches veteran classification on one's 40th birthday, so I was well qualified for this particular event.

The second and third stages were to be road races, a discipline I had not explored before. So now I was set to become a stage racer.

Again, the venue was the familiar Glyn Neath environs and the weather was, well, need I say more?

Let me just state that we are in South Wales – enough said? The first two stages were to take place on the Saturday with the third and final stage on the Sunday. To compete in the Sunday stage one had to complete the two stages on Saturday. Sounds simple.

I rode the stage one 3-mile time trial which I found tough, as it was mostly uphill on an undulating course, and after a couple of hours rest I lined up for stage two, a road race which comprised three laps of an 8-mile circuit.

The peloton, which was about 15 strong, set off at a very leisurely cadence and rode together for the whole of the first circuit, with no-one extending themselves in the slightest. We thus completed lap 1 and set off for the second, which was where my tactical knowhow was yet again to let me down big style. This, my debut race on the road, was about to blow up in my face.

I had watched the breakaway riders in the professional peloton strut their stuff, and I had always thought that if I was a road racer, then that would be my chosen strategy. So without looking round, I broke from the peloton, and stamping on the pedals, started to open up a gap. When I did finally look round the rest of the peloton seemed as though they were out on a Sunday club run so I pressed on some more, surmising that this just might be the race-winning move on my part.

After about five minutes another cursory glance to the rear told me that they were still the same distance adrift of me, about 2 to 300 metres behind, so I relaxed and started to tap out a comfortable rhythm, which would see me maintain my gain. Not a bit of it. A cycling nanosecond later I suddenly heard a whirring noise behind me, and before I could look round, the whole of the peloton swept past in the blink of an eye and quickly opened up a gap of about 200 metres on me, the erstwhile pacesetter, who had been left totally unprepared in the distance. And what's more they were pulling further away.

When I finally gathered my senses I tried to respond, but there was nothing left in my legs and my fellow veterans were fast disappearing way up the road. So, with my tail between my legs, I completed the second circuit and promptly climbed off, thereby abandoning the race. This meant of course that I would not be allowed to start the third stage the following day, so I got into my car and drove away, completely and utterly chastened.

Following on from the previous paragraph, I have perpetrated other acts of cycling idiocy which spring readily to mind, such as when I cleated in on my right pedal before the start of a race, and not being held up at that precise moment by the pusher-off, I over-balanced and landed in a tangled heap at the starter's feet, to the delight of my co-testers behind me in the queue.

I have turned up for a race without my cycling shoes, meaning that I have had to compete in my trainers with their slippery soles. I have also forgotten my aero helmet on another occasion, when I was forced to borrow another rider's road helmet, both being acts which probably add about three minutes to your race time.

On another occasion I was the penultimate starter for a 25 in the depths of Somerset, and the problem I encountered here needs a little explanation. This was an Open Time Trial, a race run by a club for which entries from the riders are closed up to a fortnight before race day. The start sheet is produced well in advance of the race, based on the current and previous records at the relevant race distance of the entrants.

The race organiser will then place the participants in blocks of five, allocating the perceived best rider in that group a seeded position. This has the effect of anyone whose race number ends in a '0' or a '5' being a seeded rider, and in theory they should overtake everyone preceding them in their block of five during the actual race, right up to the next seeded rider. In practice, the best entrant on time and/or reputation will go off last of all.

I hope I have explained all that succinctly, because back in deepest Somerset I was the last but one rider, with only that day's express train (or race favourite) to start behind me. I had never seen this course before, so would be relying on the race marshalling to get me out and back safely. The express train would of course overtake me almost as soon as I had cleated in and turned my first pedal, so I would be the last rider on the road throughout the event, unless somebody in front of me became sick of the palsy and I was chosen by fate to be able to overtake them.

We set off, and as always on an unfamiliar course, you look for local landmarks which will confirm you are on the correct path in the second half of the race when these landmarks reappear in your sight. Things went according to expectations. At the start the express train quickly left me for dead and shot off rapidly into the distance, fast becoming a blur and then disappearing from view altogether. The next time I would see him was when he would be relaxing back at the race HQ euphemistically smoking his pipe and wearing his carpet slippers, as he recounted to anyone who would be listening how he won the race without theoretically breaking sweat. That was no problem.

The first roundabout we came to on the course had several exits, and it needed the marshal to point me to the correct exit for my onward journey. So far so good. It was a pleasant day for racing weather-wise for once in a while, and I was feeling good. In the closing stages of the race I reapproached the aforementioned roundabout about a mile and a half from the finish, and looked up to see that there was no marshal anywhere to be seen. I remembered with some alarm that this island had several exits and I wasn't sure which one to take, so I made a hurried selection and hared off down the road for the run in to the finish.

But something wasn't right. The scenery looked totally unfamiliar and I surmised that I had chosen the wrong exit at the roundabout. Panicking, I rapidly executed a U-turn and shot back to the roundabout to be faced with the same dilemma. Which exit would get me back onto the right course? I made another uneducated guess, choosing an exit and put my head down yet again.

This time I felt I was in more familiar territory, and I was relieved to see the finishing line fast approaching. But now the timekeeper was on his feet with his back to the road, packing up his folding chair and chequered flag so that he could get back to HQ with the riders' times.

As I passed him, I yelled my number as the race rules demanded whilst traversing the finishing line. Whereupon he shot round, and asked the silliest question of the day "Where have you come from?". I slammed my brakes on and swung round, informing him in an extremely narked voice that the marshal had packed up and disappeared at the previous roundabout, causing me to go the wrong way.

He retorted that he knew the marshal had packed up, because the errant official had told him that there were no more riders on the road. "Bloody Nora!" was about the most apposite comment I could come up with at this juncture, and accordingly I harrumphed my way back to HQ, muttering that in true Falklands War fashion someone should have counted us all out and counted us all back.

By the time I got back to the HQ I had calmed down a little, but my health and temper was not improved when I discovered that my race time had not been recorded by the finishing official and furthermore, being the last rider on the road by some minutes, all the bloody cakes had been eaten by the rest of the riders, most of whom probably were now safely back at home tucked up in bed. I can't stomach incompetence.

Which brings me onto another recurring problem I have encountered during my time trialling career thus far.

Not mechanical issues as you might think, the threat of a race-ending puncture being ever present, but that of riding a course for the first time and taking the wrong turning. I have several instances of this on my charge sheet, unfortunately.

One I recall was on a course in the southern part of Worcestershire, on the country lanes near to the Strensham service station on the M5. This particular 10-mile course involved a series of left-hand turns which bring you back out on to the A road from whence battle had commenced, and then the charge to the finish would be along this road.

There was, I was reliably informed by the gathering riders before the start, a sharp turn in one hamlet which could easily be missed, so I was to lookout for the sign for Joe's Garage and an arrow pointing the way to a 90° left turn. I enquired as to whether this turn was being marshalled, and was told that as there weren't enough helpers to man the whole course that night it wasn't being marshalled, but not to worry, you can't miss it.

Now, whenever anyone says to me that I can't miss it, you can safely bet a pound to a penny that not only will I miss it, but I will be the only rider to do so. Just in case of uncertainty I did what I always did, and enquired of the starter and the pusher-off by way of back-up for their version of the course directions.

So off I went and swiftly got into a good rhythm, making the first two turns comfortably and continuing my onward progress. I found myself in the hamlet where Joe's Garage should have been beckoning, and saw nothing remotely resembling an arrow pointing left. Therefore I carried on. And on.

And on.

Eventually I came to the A road I was looking for but a signpost advised me that I was now nearer to Evesham than to Worcester, which certainly wasn't where I needed to be, and as I had already done 11 miles, then it was safe to assume I had gone the wrong way.

As I was totally oblivious of the correct way to go, I decided that the safest plan was to retrace my tyre tracks and head back to the start. Which I did, reaching the site (and my car) after riding 20 miles in total and with the daylight starting to fail.

One unlucky club official had been deputed to wait there for me in his car as the whole crew of the race organisers were now scattered around the time trial course scouring the county for me. I thought "Thanks, boys, for a wonderfully-organised race!". And to complicate matters further, I drove home with my race number still attached to my skinsuit, so I was forced to post it back to the race-organising club.

It is a mind-numbing experience to suddenly discover that you have taken the wrong turn in a race, as it renders your whole effort, around which you have planned your day, totally futile. I always seem to be the rider who misses the "hidden signpost" at the moment my navigational skills fail to function properly; and it almost always occurs during a race in which I am going well.

I have also turned up for races at the wrong venue, as well as appearing on completely the wrong day. I have arrived for a club time trial, for which you enter on the start line, devoid of the cash for which I need to pay to enter; and have had to negotiate a ride by virtue of the surety of my grizzled features, and a promise to pay next time.

I am Cycling Time Trials equivalent of a character from the "Viz" comic book, whose name cannot be written in these pages because of its sweary content, but those of you familiar with that publication will know to whom I am referring! Just call me Terry!

One race saw me on a very challenging course in West Sussex, one which is difficult to ride because of its uphill sections that always disrupt the rhythm of your cadence. I had thought long and hard about this route, and had mentally figured out where I was going to be making my efforts to combat and conquer its switchback nature. I was going really well, but was perplexed as the elapsed time showing on my handlebar computer was evaporating swiftly up to and beyond my targeted course best.

I was totally confused as I sped through the finishing line over two minutes slower than my previous best time for this nightmare ride. As I looked down at my computer, I immediately observed that my front chain ring was on the smaller of the two chain rings and I had therefore ridden the second half of the race in a very low gear, which explained the evaporating time. The poor condition of the road, rutted and potholed at roughly the halfway stage over a two-mile stretch, had bounced the chain off the big ring and I hadn't even noticed. I was really annoyed at this occurrence as I had wasted good conditions through no fault of my own. As Fred Flintstone would say – "Doh!"

I used to ride a 10-miler on the A38 in Somerset which is a course I have always loved. Set in the hinterland behind Weston-Super-Mare, the route starts 50 metres off the main road outside the cottage where the late legendary comedian Frankie Howerd lived for the final 30 years of his life with his partner. When I moved back to Birmingham, I still used to ride this course whenever I could and quite often the races were scheduled on summer Saturday evenings.

One day about five years ago I gave myself an exhilarating Saturday by riding in two races on the same day with the venues 100 miles apart. Both races were Open events, so I had to pay and enter these races 10 days in advance, which meant I was committed financially to my double-header. And two 10-milers only add up to 20 miles of racing; with a gap of about four hours in between there was ample sensible time for recovery, which time would all be spent seated in the car. 20 miles in two chunks of 10 miles separated by four hours is nothing when I race over 25, 30, 50 and even 100-mile time trials.

The first race was on my beloved K33/10 course in the Vale of Evesham, and the weather was glorious as I completed the first test.

Then I signed off, had my fill of tea, cake and biscuits, of course, and packed everything back into the car for the onward trip to Somerset.

Once I arrived there, in plenty of time, I walked into the tiny village hall to sign on and was confronted with the sight of Luke Rowe, who is now the road captain of Team INEOS (formerly Team Sky) and leads that great team in the Tour de France, making many of their racing decisions on the hoof (mixed metaphor alert!) during those gruelling stages. Luke is also the youngest son of Courtney Rowe, who coached me and my brother through our track accreditation course on the boards at Newport Velodrome.

I have always been starstruck, and I watched everything he did in preparation before I noticed on the signing on sheet that Luke Rowe was going to ride the race twice, being the first rider off and also the last.

His status accorded him that privilege, as he was obviously using the event as part of his own training regime, probably while he was having a few days away from the spotlight with his family in Cardiff.

Timing my warm up to the start perfectly so that I could watch him set off and accelerate through his first half mile or so, boy, did he look good? Tanned and lean, with his back as straight as a spirit level he looked a role model for scrubbers like me to copy.

I looped around and thought I could get myself positioned nicely to watch him finish, which I did, and he recorded some outrageous time of around or just under 20 minutes.

Then it was my turn to race, and off I went on a course I love and feeling good despite already having one eyeballs-out effort in my legs from earlier in the day. It is a CTT rule, which is enforced strictly, that a competitor cannot warm up on the race route once the time trial has started, but that rule was relaxed on that day for Luke Rowe, and as I was powering along the A38, yes, eyeballs out, Luke cruised past me on his warm down!

That put me firmly into my place, but I didn't really mind as he and I were sharing the road for a brief minute or so.

Anyway, I completed my second ride of the day feeling absolutely brilliant, and asking myself whether or not I could ride double headers more often, particularly in glorious weather like this. This was merely another example of the enormous pleasure one can derive from time trialling. And yes, I was into the cakes and biscuits to make it a true double header. (You can see why I have struggled with the old avoirdupois over the years, can't you?)

I recently rode in a Christmas time trial down in Hampshire where fancy dress was encouraged, turning out in bright red Santa pyjamas, with electronic (working) fairy lights attached to my aero helmet. I was beaten to the 1st prize for the fancy dress, for which at most there were three entrants out of a total of about 20 riders, by a couple in their seventies riding a tandem who wore school uniform; she a pleated skirt, school blouse and tie, he a kilt, school shirt and tie.

On a freezing morning they covered this lot up with other outer garments to keep warm during the race, during which we rode through a sleet storm. I was true to my fancy dress and rode throughout the wintry conditions in full festive regalia.

The fancy dress prize was £25, which would have covered my expenses for the day, including the cost of my pyjamas, but I am sure the couple on the tandem were deserved winners as members of the organising club, of which I was not. Sour grapes? You bet your cotton socks it was! I left there convinced I could have ridden stark naked and no-one would have noticed.

I have, though, actually won three time trials in my 552 race career, and the first one was achieved in 2015 against all the odds. Please let me explain. We were racing one Sunday on a 10-mile course close to Knowle, Warwickshire on a freezing morning and I and two other hardy souls were the only riders with the bottle to brave the conditions. I was the oldest of the trio of riders, conceding 10 and

20 years to the other two competitors. I was number 1 on the line and so started the proceedings.

On this particular course, if you get it right, there are some very fast stretches before you encounter a technical stretch covering the last couple of miles. These involve slaloming through a bridge and a very sharp 90° final left turn into the finishing lane. I reached the bridge and felt that small tell-tale bump in my front tyre which miserably signified I had run over something sharp and sustained a puncture.

Glancing at the computer on my handlebars I had about one mile to go, and decided that as my car was parked at the finishing line anyway, I might as well limp there on my injured bike as best I could. I reached the final turn and crawled my way over the closing 200 metres to take the chequered flag. The group of officials spotted I had a problem by virtue of my lack of speed across the line so I settled down to wait for the following riders to take their one and two minutes out of me.

But a full minute elapsed and there was no sign of rider number two, so I had at least defeated him.

And then incredibly the second minute ticked by and there was no sign of either of them, so I was the winner, despite puncturing! Suddenly they both came around the corner after about two and a half minutes but I was already doing my television interviews by then! My prize for this victory against all the odds? A cup of tea and an extra milk chocolate digestive biscuit. But it was worth it, what a great feeling.

My second victory was achieved in 2019 and again in a three-hander on a tricky course at Ockley in Surrey. My rivals were someone who was even older than me, and another guy returning from injury, but as I won by over 5 and 10 minutes I will back myself against them any day!

My third and to date, final victory was achieved a week before the Coronavirus lockdown began, so I entered that critical phase in top form. Just my luck. This was a four-hander in Surrey so it was the first time I have won a race with more than three competitors. Marginal gains *par excellence*!

I have had one glorious experience which may (or may not) have escaped the notice of the cycling cognoscenti in that in 2009 I became the 60 to 64 age group National Champion of Wales at 25 miles. How so? I hear you incredulously enquire. Well, let me tell you.

I entered the Welsh 25-mile Time Trial Championship on the familiar Llandovery to Carmarthen course and all the age groups would provide a winner who would of course win the medal as National (age group) Champion. Here is where the story becomes more believable, there were only me and two others in my category. Needless to say, I whipped them both and took my first National title (and only one to date). The important words in that last sentence are 'to date'. Positive thinking.

I waited patiently for the winter to arrive when I would be presented with my medal, but in the meantime the Welsh Time Trial Association, or whatever their name was, went bust. The Prize Winners' Gala presentation Ball and Dinner, or whatever they had got arranged never took place and I have little back-up to the story I have just regaled. But I was Welsh National Champion, honest!

With my newly discovered prowess of climbing hills (and mountains) for the first time in the 2019 season I took a full part in the traditional end-of-season hill climb time trials, which litter the racing calendar from mid-August to the end of the season, coming at around the end of British Summer Time. I tried one hill climb, found I could complete it, and carried on entering them. By definition they are not pleasant experiences, but there is a massive sense of achievement when you reach the finishing line as you have just raced, yes raced, up the gradients without flinching.

Hill climbers are a breed apart, but I am pleased to report that I have joined the ranks through my own hard work. My very first hill climb time trial was in early August 2019, only a week after I had conquered Alpe d'Huez. As usual, I waited with shredded nerves in the queue at the start as I hadn't a clue as to what to expect when I began my debut ascent, but what did actually occur took me completely off guard.

After I had pedalled no more than two to three hundred metres, I felt the usual runny nose sensation which meant the back of my cycling mitt would soon be coming into play. What are gloves for after all? But the running of the nose is usually reserved for cold mornings, and when I wiped my nose I glanced at my glove and saw it covered in blood. I had chosen the most inopportune moment to have a nosebleed, but just as boxers do, I carried on with my nose bleeding and completed the climb. What a trooper! I am pleased to report however that I have not had a recurrence of that particular problem!

I had a real hard luck story in the season of 2016 when I entered the Tour of Cambridgeshire, which is a two-day festival of cycle racing centred on the Peterborough Showground. Day one consists of a closed road 16- mile time trial and day two a road race. Both of these carry automatic entry for the first three riders home in each five-year age category to represent Great Britain in the time trial and road race World Championships, which that year were scheduled to take place in Perth, Western Australia.

There were about 20 riders in my age group, the 65-69 category, and the course was a challenging, technical mixture of uphills and fast sections. I rode off early morning from the raised podium inside the hall which was to double as the HQ, and that in itself was quite a thrilling experience, as it replicated how the professionals start time trials during stage races.

Although it was midsummer (I recall it may have been Derby day) the early weather felt freezing cold, but I soon got myself warmed up with what was turning into a good productive ride.

As the roads were closed to traffic, the final section within the actual grounds of the Showground itself were barriered, and there were a couple of thousand spectators and riders there to welcome you at the finish after you had snaked through a Tour de France-style finishing chute.

I was correct in that I had ridden well, but was a little disappointed to find that I had finished fourth and so didn't make the automatic qualification places. However, if anyone in the first three declined their offer of a place in the World Championships, then you were moved up a place in the rankings, and a few days later I was contacted by an email from the organisers who advised me that finishers two and three had dropped out (presumably because of the huge logistical problem and the cost of decamping to Australia for just one race); and I was therefore offered a place.

As luck would have it, I couldn't go either for the same reasons, and so had to forego what would have been a memorable occasion. It seems slightly incongruous that if you qualify to represent your country at a world championship event then you have to foot the bill personally. Ah well, nothing that a large-sized Lottery win wouldn't take care of. I didn't hang around for the next day's road race, as I would have been sunk without trace in that company. The secret of this type of age-group racing is to concentrate your effort in the years when you are the newcomer to your category, i.e. the youngest. So we will see what the coming years bring as I haven't given up hope of qualifying.

One always gets a bit of a sinking feeling when overtaken during a time trial, and at my age, as either one of the oldest or quite often the oldest rider in the race, this can happen frequently. As the rider goes past me I do a quick mental calculation. For example, if someone has taken two minutes out of me at the halfway stage then they are on target to beat me by four minutes. So if the final gap at the finish between us is, say, only three minutes, then that is an indication of how much better I rode during the second half of the race.

This could be due to how good I was feeling, the terrain being more sympathetic, or the wind direction changing from a head to a tailwind, or a combination of all three factors.

Now and then I actually overtake someone (yes, honestly!), and this is a great feeling, particularly if you have targeted someone before the race. You can get into a real ding-dong battle when you are overtaken, then you claw the deficit back and go past them, and there may be a repeat. Whilst it is against the rules of time trialling to draught behind a rider, that is to say obtain the benefit of the shelter from the wind that they are providing and riding in their slipstream, there is nothing illegal about overtaking again someone who has just perpetrated the evil deed on you. These tit-for-tat battles are exhilarating to be a part of, and at the chequered flag it nearly always leads to me and my rival, both exhausted and full of adrenalin, congratulating each other on a most enjoyable race.

I have ridden three time trials over the exacting distance of 100 miles, all on the same course in South Wales. The course runs along the dual carriageways between Abergavenny, that wonderful cycling town, and Monmouth, along the A40. There and back three times, totalling the full distance of a ton of miles. The course undulates, but not seriously, and there are some quick stretches on which to periodically extend your legs.

For my age the Veterans Time Trialling Association (the VTTA) birthday-related handicapping system gives me a standard time a smidgeon short of five hours, and I have beaten this significant target each time, recording a PB of just under four and a half hours.

On the first occasion I attempted this daunting distance I hadn't a clue how to plan it, as I had no real experience to fall back on. So I simply broke the race up into five-mile segments once it got going, and using my mental arithmetic skills calculated what my pro rata finishing time would be, and whether I was slowing up or improving on it as each section flew by. These calculations, which became more taxing to my brain as the figures got bigger and bigger, helped me to pass the time and thereby alleviate any tedium I might have been experiencing from so long a time in the saddle.

It is surprising, however, that if you are fit enough then you can definitely ride the distance eyeballs-out and have an enormously satisfying day out on the bike. The first 100- miler was when I achieved my PB, as I haven't been able to better it in my two subsequent attempts. Just as I had crossed the finishing line on that auspicious day and I was gently riding back to my car at HQ, one of my clubmates from the Oggies rode past me in the other direction, and said something in passing to me which I didn't quite pick up.

Turning to look back and see if it was possible to continue the conversation, I wasn't able to uncleat in time and promptly deposited myself and my bike on the floor, prompting all around me to think I had collapsed with exhaustion, when in fact I had collapsed with embarrassment!

I feel sure that if I ever win BBC Sports Personality of the Year (Odds against that happening? Several million to one. Get a shilling on me now!) I would probably trip up on the final step to the stage and stagger forward and headbutt Gary Lineker in the groin, all captured in glorious technicolor on BBC Television. Worth voting for me just to see if I could accomplish that feat with the famed crisp advertiser!

Delirium is a constant adversary of all who pit their wits against the clock in a time trial. I always seem to doubt my sanity whenever I ride a 30-mile race in the Shropshire countryside near Market Drayton. This course is a standard 15 out-15 back and the first half is usually accompanied by a favourable westerly tailwind, which is lovely, except that the incline is still predominantly upward. Then you reach the turn and you think that now the gradient will be predominantly downhill, but you constantly seem to suffer because there is a headwind slowing your progress.

Each time I have ridden this course I say the same thing at the finish to anyone who is prepared to listen, that I am sure this course is uphill in both directions. Fellow riders nod in compliant agreemen,t and then move away to the cakes and biscuits nudging each other that they are all on nutter alert! I wouldn't mind but it isn't even a difficult course. Delirium.

Despite evidence to the contrary I keep myself very much to myself at races, as I still feel like a newcomer to the sport, and this makes me a little bashful. At cricket particularly I was exactly the opposite due to my constant involvement in the game from the age of eight, which at times meant that my big mouth could run away with me. I hated myself for that trait and I hope those days are long gone.

However, I remain a keen observer of my fellow man, and whether I am competing in South Wales, the Midlands or my new home region of London South I have riders whom I target on race days. I will give no hints as to who these people are, other than to say that privately they have got my hackles up through either their own arrogance, or a mistaken estimation of their own ability, or in one or two cases, they have been simply downright rude to me.

The latter is anathema to me as my late Mom would attest, as I still believe earnestly that manners maketh man. So, if I am racing against any of these unnamed characters, then I have a secret peep at the results board after the race to see whether I have put them in their place. And if I haven't, I say to myself that next time Sonny Jim, you are going down. (Ignore me, I will soon go away).

Usually through no fault of my own (he says!) I always seem to ride at my best when I am angry. But I don't get myself worked up deliberately, having become increasingly more laid back as I further misspend my dotage. However, some things really hack me off, such as not being able to find the venue of a race or getting there late so that I have no time to warm up. I once had to drive in my car to park at the start for a time trial in which all my pre-race time had elapsed. I got out of the car with less than two minutes to spare to my start time, so my warm up consisted of a slow freewheel of about ten yards! Doesn't do much for the muscles but works wonders for the health, temper and adrenalin production!

Occasionally the race organisers will hack me off with their rudeness or an uncooperative nature, and even more rarely when a fellow competitor has been rude, arrogant or dismissive to me. All combine to make me an angry rider and I suppose I take it out on the bike.

"Never leave anything on the bike" in terms of effort is the competitive cyclist's mantra anyway, so it all helps to get me wound up to race speed and effort.

A couple of years ago compulsory drug-testing was introduced to CTT events, and lest we forget, we are an amateur sport. But the usage of drugs is apparently rife even in our branch of the sport. I can think of someone, and I will give no clues as to his identity for fear of his lawyers bombarding me with writs, who is notorious for his use of banned substances, and he is a serial winner. You can easily recognise him however, as he glows in the dark!

Not every time trial is drug-tested however, but the drug squad will present themselves unannounced on the day of an event, and they have to be given complete freedom to carry out their duties. They will announce before the start of the races the numbers of the riders that they wish to drug test, randomly selected (of course!) and display those selected numbers clearly on the start sheet, so that there will be no confusion as to who is to be tested. If one fails to comply, either by clearing off home or simply plain refusing to cooperate, then that is seen as a positive test and you will be susceptible to a suspension.

I rode in just such a race in Leicestershire in the first year of these tests and (let us say I was number 48) number 49, or my minute man, was selected for the dreaded post-race test. Phew! That was a narrow escape, although I would probably have tested positive for EPO. Don't be alarmed, I am not referring to the banned substance Erythropoietin, known in the trade as EPO. No sir, in my case EPO stands for Extra Porridge Oats! Mind you, if porridge does ever sneak onto the list of banned substances, then my career is down the toilet straight away! I digress. Not like me at all.

Anyway, I rode my race which, of course, took place on a bitterly cold day which was accompanied by a deluge of extremely unpleasant rain, so nothing new under the sun there. What sun? As the conditions were so unpleasant, I collected my top from the starter nearby after I crossed the finishing line so that I could ride back to HQ in relative warmth and comfort.

HQ was at a local school, and when I rode into the school drive I was confronted by the drug testers. As I was not one of the selected riders, I pedalled complacently past them only to hear a booming "Stop!" ringing in my ears. As we finish in roughly the same numerical order as we started then they obviously thought I was number 49 and I had covered my number up with my raintop.

"What number are you?" "F-f-forty eight" I stammered as I shivered, fearing a Gestapo-like interrogation was coming my way, and I revealed my previously concealed number to them. "Oh, that's OK. Please proceed." I dread to think what they would do to any uncooperative testee. It was with some trepidation I got stuck into my biscuits and cake that afternoon I can tell you!

I think this particular race was jinxed because the following year the men's and women's events were separated with the men going off first and the ladies much later. This time there were no drug testers to be seen. The men rode their race, which commenced at 2 p.m. and I was one of the later riders finishing at about 3.30.

As I started back to HQ, I noticed that the sky was turning a weird purple colour which obviously heralded something nasty for the women who were due to start at 4 p.m. I was safely back at HQ biscuitting and caking when the heavens opened, and the purple sky unleashed a blizzard of sleet and snow which had the school car park covered in a matter of minutes. The women riders stood at the windows gloomily bemoaning their fate but it quickly became obvious that they would be spared this ordeal and their race was cancelled.

The only problem was that the start and finish officials were probably at best sat in their cars waiting for it to blow over or at worst sat huddled under umbrellas in the open air rapidly turning into snowmen. But thanks to the modern miracle of the mobile phone they were recalled and very soon they tucked into what I had left of the biscuits and cakes.

I did have a brush with a possible ban however in 2019 when I had a very strange exchange of emails with a race organiser.

I had ridden a 10-miler on a very fast course in Hertfordshire, no more details than that will be provided to protect the rude! The time trial itself was fine, but as I was on the 60-mile journey back home I realised that my race number was still attached to my skinsuit, a schoolboy error.

Nothing I could do about the situation so I posted it back to the sponsoring club with a note of apology the moment I returned home, because as previously stated, manners maketh man.

Imagine my surprise when the race organiser himself (I doff my cap to you, sir!) emailed me about two weeks later, not to thank me for returning my number, but to tell me that he had video evidence of me warming up on the actual race route after the race had started, which is a serious breach of CTT rules and that he was considering recommending me to the governing body for a suspension from racing! I was apoplectic with rage on receiving this message.

What I had actually done was this: before the race to get to the start, I had ridden to the nearest part of the course that I knew, which was a roundabout at the seven-mile mark, and continued to pedal sedately to the start along the last three miles of the course itself, which was a live racing course by the time I circumnavigated the roundabout. I quite seriously didn't think that there was any other way of actually reaching the start line other than by this route.

It transpired that there was another route, which I rode in reverse after the finish by following other finishers back to the HQ. I will not print this bloke's name but will tab him Josiah Jobsworth, for the sake of clarity, or JJ for short. So I had a think, and while I hadn't exactly calmed down I reasoned that I had to do something here or I was going to cop a suspension, which for me would have been tantamount to a disaster.

I emailed JJ back and pointed out that if he looked at his precious video then he would see that I was merely touring to the start and not 'warming up' which would have seen me in the aero 'tuck' position and simulating race conditions. And furthermore, if he wanted to recommend me for a suspension then go right on ahead and do it. It would make him feel as though he had justified his own miserable existence, he could then feel proud of himself that he had deprived a quite innocent racing cyclist of his hobby, and thereby actively prevented him from participating in the thing that he loved doing, and furthermore I was an amateur funding my own racing.

I deliberately ladled it on as thickly as possible, but if I had met him face to face I would have unloaded verbally on him with both barrels at his threat to my racing participation; which, in retrospect, would have guaranteed me an instant suspension pending a personal hearing.

Boy I was angry, but lo and behold, I have not received a further response from JJ to this day, so I hope this miserable baggage of a race organiser saw the error of his ways and closed my particular file with immediate effect. For once, my reaction to authority, which has been (unjustifiably) downright contemptuous over the years worked in my favour this time and saw justice done, although I would say that wouldn't I?

I try to race as often as I can these days, as the realisation dawns that I am not getting any younger and only God knows when the time will come to ring down my own racing curtain. This attitude saw me race a record 80 time trials during the 2016 season, and in 2019 I set out to beat that number. Starting with the Brighton Excelsior 10-miler on New Year's Day I began my quest for the magic number of 81 events. However, a combination of repeatedly lousy weather causing cancellations, me going to the wrong venue, and riding off course, coupled with inconveniently arranged holiday dates meant that I fell short and had to admit defeat with 75 in the book. At the time of writing, which is January 2020, I have set off again and I am actually targeting the figure of 100 time trials in one season. This is another challenge that won't see me rest until I have achieved it.

Some fellow riders get involved in my quest for numbers, and as we exchange small talk in the starting queues, they frequently enquire what number today's event is in my cumulative calendar, and it is nice to share a little personal something like that. This relentless chase after races has seen me clock up a personal record of nine time trials in nine days, and I have also done six in six and seven in seven.

Incredibly I don't find it tiring, as I am obviously at a fitness level which keeps me topped up, buzzing and raring to ride. What a great feeling it is, and at my age too!

My 500th time trial was ticked off during 2019 and as luck would have it, it was over 50 miles, a distance I hadn't taken on since before my racing accident in 2017. The terrain got harder and harder and by the time I reached the finishing funnel for my own private celebration I was all in.

When I came to climb off my bike my right groin seized and I could barely move, and this discomfort was a precursor to an identical injury I was to suffer at the summit of Alpe d'Huez some eight weeks later. It was caused by staying in one position all the time in the saddle so the sudden movement to dismount caused the muscle to seize up and give me a very uncomfortable couple of days. You would think I would have factored this in when I climbed the Alp, wouldn't you? Still, 500 down and on to the next 500 races, which at the current rate of progress will be close to my 80th birthday. Seriously, that fact is true!

Of course, some races unavoidably end in personal disaster, such as when your bike sustains a mechanical problem which prevents any further forward momentum. I have had, and will continue to have, no doubt, just like every other racer, a puncture thankfully once in a while when a time trial has started. There is nothing you can do about this misfortune, so it is game over for that particular day. You can't carry a puncture repair kit or a spare inner tube and a pump to repair the hole and get you back to HQ, because you minimise the weight you carry during the event – remember less weight equals free speed – so you just hope you can either limp back on your wounded steed, or be picked up by the broom wagon. This is a vehicle which drives the course after the last rider has been pushed off, in order to ensure that there are no stragglers suffering mechanical issues that need dealing with; or, heaven forbid, somebody has crashed and could be requiring ugent medical attention.

Talking of the broom wagon, I have only one experience of it, which was when I was competing in the famous Dragon Ride, which is a lengthy tour of South Wales where several thousand cyclists from all around the UK descend on the start. This is a massive logistical operation for the organisers, who not only have to try and ensure everyone gets round the Principality and home safely, but any riders who don't are swept up and transported back to the HQ in the official vehicle.

In one particular year, this was me. I punctured, as luck would have it, about 65 miles from the finish line, and I had to stand by the roadside until the broom wagon, which was a large minibus, turned up and me and my bike were placed inside. I was the only rider the vehicle had collected who hadn't been involved in a crash and there were broken bodies lying everywhere in the van. We even saw two riders ahead of us crash into each other, and I was one of those who helped them and their mangled bikes into the bus. Not an experience I really wish to repeat on a regular basis, but an essential service, nonetheless.

The cycling-friendly television channel ITV4 broadcast highlights every year of a series of 10 criteria (town centre races over closed roads) known as The Tour Series, which are competed for by all the top British professional teams. This is a magnificent spectacle, and the broadcasting channel do a superb job in bringing this to our TV screens. The series is shoehorned into the month of May, and to me it heralds the fact that the racing season is now full on. I love these races, and in 2014 one of the rounds of the Tour Series was held in the town centre of Redditch in Worcestershire, about 15 miles from Birmingham.

The course is about a mile and a quarter long, and is completely closed to traffic and barriered off over its full length. Before the men's and women's races took place a time trial over one lap was held, and entry was online on a first come first served basis. I entered and got in.

I turned up on the night with my brother in tow as my Directeur Sportif and we were accosted, if that is the right word, by a journalist from Cycling Weekly, the one and only comic itself, who interviewed us both as to how we approached time trialling.

I muttered something in response and a photographer snapped us both. To my utter amazement in next week's edition of the comic there was our picture, accompanied by a few quotes.

The time trial itself was an absolute bloody nightmare. The course went from a rapid downhill descent, through a 90°left turn, an uphill stretch and then a finishing wall (a very steep hill) which led to a flat finishing strait of about 100 metres. I lost my momentum completely and recorded a lousy time; beating I recall, a couple of kids in diapers on balance bikes, it felt that bad. And all in front of a growing crowd which touched an estimated 10,000. Thankfully the TV cameramen were having a cuppa and a fag while I was racing, if you can call what I was doing racing.

Of course, the professional riders, male and female, go on later to make total mincemeat of this course, and the TV pictures do not reveal to the viewer what a challenging circuit this is.

But this wasn't the only time I appeared in Cycling Weekly. Oh no! After I had completed my first 12 months in the saddle in September 2008, I felt moved to write to the comic extolling the pleasure that I had taken from this achievement and the life-changing circum-stances that I was experiencing. To my delight they published my letter in the very next edition, with Friday being publication day.

The following day, the Saturday (for those who haven't memorised the sequence of the days of the week) I was halfway through a day's ride around South Wales and had stopped for a cup of tea and an ice cream at a sea front café in Porthcawl, that lovely resort town. I was wearing my full Oggies kit, and I heard a voice behind me asking me if I was Brian Jones!

I swung round to see an elderly couple sat at the table behind me and I owned up and said that I was indeed the aforementioned. The gentleman said I guessed you might be as I have just read your letter in Cycling Weekly and you mentioned in it that you are an Oggie. What were the chances?

Seizing on my new found fame, or notoriety, we engaged in conversation and it turned out he was a former member of the Oggies, and indeed the current chairman of the club had been best man at their wedding! I love coincidences and this was jaw-droppingly special. Of all the cafes in all the world, I should cycle into this one! We parted company eventually and I rode on buoyed by this wonderful experience, thinking to myself, do I now need an agent? Delusions of grandeur indeed.

I have also ridden in front of a crowd of a few thousand people several times at Blenheim Palace, in Woodstock, Oxfordshire. A festival of cycling used to be held in the grounds of the Palace each autumn, and one of the events was a time trial which was raced over three circuits around the wooded environs of the palace. The circuit isn't particularly flat, but one's reward came as the finishing funnel was barriered off, and thousands of spectators would throng the closing yards to give us all a huge thrill as we finished.

After about five successive years of this festival the Palace authorities discontinued the event, because they felt the thousands of spectators weren't visiting the innerds of the Palace enough. Too right, they were there for a festival of cycling.

So, a great event in the cycling calendar, which also included the Brompton World Championship, this being raced in full businesswear, i.e jackets, shirts and ties for the men or blouses and jackets for the ladies, was lost due to a completely illogical decision, taken by a body of people who obviously disliked cycling and cyclists.

There is a school of thought that says in any time trial you shouldn't burn your boats and go full on from the gun, as you won't have any reserves for the final push. I don't subscribe to that theory as I prefer to ride a 10-mile time trial full on, eyeballs out, and leave nothing on the bike at the chequered flag. What is the point in crossing the line and feeling that you could have gone quicker because you husbanded your resources during the first part of the race?

Nah, go for it, it is going to be less than a half hour of purgatory and this is what you train for, to get to your threshold and hold it there. I frequently ask myself why I am not gasping for breath and on my last legs, having to be helped off my bike at the finish.

I suspect the answer to that question is that I can push myself still harder, and one day, I will know the answer to that when I have flogged myself to within an inch of the Pearly Gates. I'm getting there, you just have to grit your teeth and ride fearlessly, which I realise is easier said than done.

CHAPTER SEVEN

Ride a Race with Me

I would like now to take you through the procedure of actually riding a time trial and how it all comes together for me, a 69-years-young racer. Because I am bald then whatever bits of stubble adorn my bonce are grey, now hence the sub-title of this tome – Grey racer!

If you are already a time triallist, then please skip this chapter or else read it for a giggle and say, "Well, that certainly isn't how I do it!".

Let us imagine it is Tuesday 15th June and I am about to enter an Open 10-mile time trial race scheduled for Saturday 26th June, situated some 30 miles or so from my home. The process all begins with the online entry on the Cycling Time Trials (CTT) website, and entry for the Open has to be emailed to the race organiser by the closing date and time of midnight 11 days (Tuesday) before the actual date of the race.

The entry form on the website is pre-populated with my personal details, which are stored under my unique CTT registration number, and contains data such as my name, address, telephone number, date of birth, emergency contact number, club and Personal Best information over the various official distances over which CTTs are raced. The race details, the course number, a graph of the course and written details of the route are also available online, together with details of the race HQ, i.e. where one meets to sign on and to change into your racing togs on the day.

One pays the requisite entrance fee by debit card online, part of which goes as a per capita levy to CTT itself, and also ensures you, the rider, are insured during the race. Pinning a race number on is evidence of that cover, and if one raced without a number and was involved in an accident, then the insurance cover would be invalidated. Once the submit button has been pressed, then your entry is electronically sent to the race organiser.

A few days before the race day the organiser will then publish online the start sheet for the race, and the riders are allocated a start time, at one-minute intervals, and this schedule must be strictly adhered to. If the race starts at, say 9 a.m., then the first rider will be pushed off at 9.01. If my start number is 48 then I will be sent off at 9.48.

The race organiser will seed the best riders and send them off at five -minute intervals from their fellow seeded riders, which means that if your race number ends in a '5' or a '0' then you are one of the chosen few. Needless to say, at my age and with my (lack of) ability then I am never seeded (except in my dreams!)

Fast forward now to the night before race day and my evening meal will usually be pasta based, as it is prudent to load in the carbs and pasta does the job adequately. Then it is sensible to get to bed at a reasonable time so that one can awaken the next morning bright-eyed and bushy-tailed, and not too tired to put in the effort because you haven't had nearly enough sleep. Good night reader, back with you in the morning.

Race day dawns. I am off at 9.48, so I will set my alarm for 6 a.m. This gives me time to crawl, sorry, bounce out of bed and start my important pre-race preparations, which are essential if I am going to give a good account of myself.

After ablutions in the bathroom which includes weighing myself, it is into the kitchen where I will have 50 grams of porridge oats, made with water and not milk, and topped off with a banana (have you seen the number of bananas tennis players consume during a match?) and a dessert spoonful of honey, for energy. To accompany my cereal I have at least one mug of black, filter coffee, to start my caffeine loading.

After breakfast, and it will now be about 6.30, I go into my diary where I have a race checklist.

This will cover what I need to wear during the race; skinsuit (which colour?), base layer, leggings (if it is likely to be chilly), socks, racing shoes with serviceable cleats and overshoes which will match the colour of my skinsuit, cycling mitts which also match my skinsuit, bandana (No, I haven't just eaten one of those) and aero helmet. I will then start to get dressed, but not before I spray my legs with a heat spray to give my muscles a warm-up boost; pain-killing gel for my poorly hands and wrists so that they don't ache during the race; drinks bottle full of electrolyte drink to replace any salts I lose during the race effort.

Next into the garage where I remove my time trial bike off its wall hanger. I will inflate my tyres using the track pump to 116 pounds per square inch, which is my desired level of inflation for road racing, and make sure I have my Garmin cycle computer (fully charged) and a working rear light, as it is now compulsory in all races these days for each rider to display one.

Finally I take my tool kit, so that I have anything I need for any last minute adjustments or fettling of the bike that I may need to do, as I do have a modicum of how to prepare my bike for a race, despite sibling opinions to the contrary! I then pack my accessories into my racing bag, and ensure that I have put in there my last bits and bobs which I will need before I leave the race HQ for the start line. Stick it all into the car after one final glance through my checklist, and then climb into the car and turn the ignition key. Off we go!

I like to arrive at a race with about 75 minutes to spare. I park up and sign on inside the HQ on the race sheet and then collect my appointed number, which in our imaginary race would be number 48.

For over 100 years cyclists and athletes have safety-pinned their numbers onto their clothing, and as a Lycra skinsuit can cost anything up to £200 then we quite ridiculously riddle it with pin holes! So now I have a genius invention of a transparent pouch in my new skinsuits where I can slide the number inside it without pins, and sensibly this new process will prolong the life and condition of any skinsuit, which owes a tremendous amount to modernity and logic, and makes my wallet an easier bedfellow!

I have two new Lycra skinsuits, one in bright green and the other in Wolverhampton Wanderers old gold, and I have matching overshoes and cycling mitts in both colours. I work on the basis that the only things that can be seen on planet Earth from Outer Space are the Great Wall of China and me on my time trial bike in one colour or the other!

I consume my last pre-race concoctions which are; two caffeine tablets for my caffeine (overdose) boost, half a packet of glucose tablets (87 calories) and an energy gel in a sachet (128 calories) and after donning my aero dynamic (pointed) helmet, I cleat myself into my pedals and I am ready to ride to the start.

At this point I like to have about 45 minutes to go before my appointed start time so that I can warm up by doing anything up to 10 miles on the way to the start which I ride at touring pace. On the way there, I may have to do a few loops to achieve the desired warm-up distance and when I have got myself there, I join the queue of riders in numerical order who are waiting to be pushed off at one-minute intervals to start their race effort.

I like to feel nicely warmed up and good to go, both mentally and physically, and there is no better feeling. It is quite relaxing to have a spot of meaningless banter with the other riders at this juncture, as it takes your mind briefly off what is about to happen. And if the truth be told, I do miss the dressing-room chat with my teammates at the cricket club.

I also make sure that my rear light is on, and flashing, now a compulsory requirement in any time trial, and that my cycle computer is reset to zero. As the clock ticks around so the butterflies increase, as your starting time approaches.

Oh, and of course, there is the last-minute dive into the bushes, as I have taken on board my fair share of black coffee that morning, and of course the black liquid is a fearsome diuretic, and, well, you know me and my bladder!

Then suddenly you are the next rider up. I should explain the consequences of being late and missing your start time. The starter will attempt to slot you back into the race by sending you off in the next available gap, which will be where someone has not taken up their entry and either not turned up on the day or sent an apology for their non-participation to the starter in advance. For example, if I missed my start at number 48 and I was sent off ten minutes later in a gap at number 58 then the 10-minute late start will be added on. In other words, my time will still be taken from 9.48! An incentive to get my timekeeping in order!

60 seconds to go, and the starter will call out your number – "Number 48" he intones and you respond by placing your front wheel on the start line. He then gives you the 30-second call and the pusher off will then hold your bike up while you cleat into the pedals and you wait as the seconds tick inexorably down.

Ten seconds – then the fingers go up in front of your face and it is "5– 4 – 3 - 2 – 1!" with a finger disappearing with each called second and then with a "Have a good ride" shout from the pusher off, you are pushed off, and away you go!

Time Trialling is known as the Race of Truth and nothing could be more accurately named. The actual truth of it is that you have to be honest with yourself and ride eyeballs out for the duration of the race. Yes, of course it hurts but this is what you have trained for and conditioned yourself to expect so your body is attuned to whatever the course throws at you.

The computer on the handlebars is logging the effort and the miles are ticking down and then you reach the last mile.

If you are familiar with the course and it is a fast finish, then you steel yourself for the final push and go for the big sprint from as far out as you can manage.

You glance up and see the chequered board which the timekeeper has placed on the finishing line, and you put your head down and blast it, yelling your race number as you "breast the tape". At last it is done, and you freewheel while your recovery begins. I like a nice two-or three-mile ride back to HQ, which serves as my warm down, and by the time I reach the car park I have got the race comfortably out of my system.

The fitter you are the quicker your recovery. The bike, helmet and shoes go back into the car and then it is straight into the HQ, which is usually a village hall, or sometimes a school, and you need to sign off on the sign-on sheet, otherwise you will be disqualified, and finally you hand back your race number.

Then comes the best part – your free cup of tea and a choice of biscuits and cake, for which one is invited to make a donation towards the cost.

As the riders finish the race their times are phoned back to HQ where they are displayed on a giant screen and you log your own time to see if the timekeeper's official version accords with your own from your cycle computer. The emotions are either disappointment, satisfaction or occasionally euphoria when your time is confirmed.

Occasionally I have won a cash prize at an Open event, which will have been for winning my age group category after the age allowances have been applied to the times. This is a rather clever handicapping system devised by the Veteran Time Triallers Association (VTTA), and is in fact an ingenious way of ensuring that every rider in the race has a chance of beating anyone else by competing on a more even playing field.

Then when you can't make any more surreptitious visits to the biscuits and cake without receiving an official reprimand, it is off home. I normally feel like a million dollars for about an hour after a race which is a lovely feeling and then I come down suddenly as fatigue hits me like a sledgehammer and then it is time for my post-race nap. I am good to go again the next day, and the next day, and the day after.

I hope you got a small flavour of why I am addicted to this majestic sport. Am I addicted to it? Yes, guilty as charged!

CHAPTER EIGHT

Le Tour de France

The Tour de France is known to French cycling fans as "Le Grand Boucle" or The Big Wheel, as the course traces a giant circle on the map.

I hold firmly that the Tour de France is the world's greatest sporting event. In July every year we, as cycling fans, are treated to the three-week spectacle of the elite road racers in the professional peloton circumnavigating le Grand Boucle over the flatlands, in the mountains and then finally, on the last day, nine laps of the Champs Elysees in the centre of Paris, the capital of France, that most beautiful and varied of countries.

If you, the reader, have never witnessed a stage of le Tour live, that is to say by actually being there, then if it is possible for you, move it straight to number one on your bucket list, highlight it then mark it with an asterisk – it is that thrilling.

One can attend the start of a stage, the finish, at a village location as the peloton speeds through in the blink of any eye, or at a mountain stage, where the riders power their way to the impossibly steep summits at a pace that does not seem humanly possible, very often standing on the pedals for periods that are not able to be replicated by mere mortals. I have done them all.

It is the biggest buzz I have ever achieved from watching a multiplicity of sports. An estimated three million spectators line the avenues, boulevards, lanes and dual carriageways of la belle France and this incomparable spectacle is free! If you are watching the live or recorded highlights on the television, it is a glorious televisual travelogue showcasing the million and one delights of the host country.

Let me recount one or two of my Tour de France escapades.

One year I attended a start in the grounds of the Chateau of Chambord, one of the astonishingly beautiful chateaux of the Loire Valley. The pathways surrounding the chateau had been barriered off to provide a course for the participants warming up prior to the roll off of the start of the stage.

The riders would gently ride around this small trackway, and occasionally pause against the barriers where they would sign autographs or chat to you if a common language could be settled upon. The team coaches would be driven into a cordoned off enclosure from where the riders would emerge, blinking into the sunshine, and begin their pre-race routines.

To obtain entry into this holy of holies, the coach park, then one needed an accreditation from the race organisers, denoting you were either a member of one of the participating teams or its entourage, a member of the press corps, or a member of the Tour organising body.

Yours truly was of course, none of those so I elected to climb the barriers when no-one was looking (at the age of 57, I ask you!) and started to mingle with the Tour hoi-polloi. I had something around my neck which was possibly an admission ticket to a menagerie I had visited the day before.

I looked across to the bus of the Italian Lampre team as it disgorged nine deeply tanned, supremely honed cyclists dressed in my favourite professional kit of royal blue and pink. I had never seen such magnificent specimens. Without troubling the Italians, I found myself in front of the door of the US Postal team bus, the team of the multiple winner Lance Armstrong, and the world's press and TV awaited his emergence from the depths of the charabanc.

This particular morning had found Armstrong in the yellow jersey for the first time on that year's tour due to the crash of the previous incumbent David Zabriskie, a fellow American, at the end of the Team Time Trial the night before at Blois.

In the time-honoured tradition Lance did not want to don the leader's jersey due to someone else's misfortune so had presented himself in his US Postal colours, only to be told by the Tour organisers that he was contractually obliged to wear it as he was the leader of the General Classification. If he disregarded these orders then he ran the risk of a fine, a time penalty or even disqualification.

He duly appeared and presented himself to the microphone and the cameras of Sky Sports TV, and he was so close to me that my chin was actually resting on his right shoulder. I felt sure he would turn and ask me to politely bugger off but to my amazement he didn't, obviously respecting my menagerie ticket more than the press accreditation the rest of the paparazzi were sporting! He duly gave a good two- or three-minute interview for the camera, and then ducked back inside the team coach to comply with orders and don le maillot jaune (yellow jersey).

Naturally I was beside myself after this occurrence and immediately texted my son back in England to enquire whether he had just watched the live interview on Sky with Lance Armstrong and whether or not he had seen my face next to the Texan's. Yes, he had watched it but as he recalled they only showed his face so my 15 minutes of fame, to paraphrase Andy Warhol, hadn't materialised. The peloton duly rolled out of Chambord in the next few minutes amid great excitement and suddenly they were gone.

I was also at a start in the French Alps in the beautiful Alpine town of Sisteron on a blisteringly hot morning, where the riders signed on in the market square on a huge, specially erected platform before lining up to be flagged on their way by the local Mayor. Here the riders are generally in a jovial mood as they chat to us, the spectators, as we are only an arm's length away.

It was here I had a brief conversation with Alberto Contador, a rider I admired greatly if only for his unique style of climbing where he just throws his bike into a low gear and stands up seemingly dancing his way up the ascents.

I wished him good luck for the day, and he responded with a cheery "thank you" having not understood a word of my Brummy accent. Probably.

Once the peloton had left town the festivities continued with a live radio show where the presenters wandered around the cafes and restaurants, conducting live interviews and playing the interviewees' favourite songs over the airwaves. All of this being broadcast simultaneously and loudly over loudspeakers, which were placed all around the town square and its environs.

I always cheekily go round the shops and cafes asking if I can have the wonderfully colourful and evocative posters advertising the great race for my own personal collection. I have to admit that I have not been averse to just nicking them off windows when no-one is looking, as very often they have been promised to other cycling fans before the great day. I know, I am a reprehensible human being, but I haven't murdered anyone. There is a brilliant atmosphere at these start towns.

When you are out in the countryside of France you may be fortunate to be near to where the peloton passes through, and this has a thrill and a charm to it as with other parts of this great race. One is advised to get to the appropriate town or village well in advance, so that you can find a convenient parking space, and also because very often the roads where the race is going to pass through are cordoned off hours before.

Then it is a question of how you spend your time as the tension begins to build. Usually one or two of the local shops will have a Tour de France themed display inside and out of their premises, and it is a great opportunity to buy Tour-themed memorabilia. Or get yourself into a local café or restaurant and sample the local foodstuffs, always a pleasant pastime. Then the Tour caravan starts to appear.

The caravan is a convoy of vehicles advertising the wares of the many companies who have sponsored le Tour. These vehicles are usually open-topped wagons which look as though they are straight out of Disneyland, adorned in the regalia of the particular sponsor and laden with pretty girls chucking out free samples, which cause a mad scramble by the spectators who are ranged six-deep at the side of the roads waiting for such booty. It is a great coup to catch something from one of the caravan wagons, and it can be something as intrinsically valuable as a 25 gramme bag of Haribo sweeties or a cardboard Tour sun visor in the General Classification leader's jersey colour of yellow.

Of greater significance is the chance that you might catch one of the actual drinks bottles cast aside (deliberately) by one of the riders as they speed by and chuck it into the crowd, causing a frantic melee as it might have been one of the better known riders who dispensed with it.

The caravan is actually several hundred vehicles long and it can take up to two hours for it to completely get through a particular town or village.

The next occurrence is the first sighting of the helicopters which are hovering over the peloton, and this raises the excitement levels to fever-pitch as the riders can now only be a couple of miles away. The helicopters provide part of the live television feeds going out all over the world. Now is the time to get your position sorted, and you clamour for a front row place against the metal barriers.

Then suddenly, the motor bikes that are escorting the peloton appear with their blue flashing lights, and now the tension is unbearable. If there is a breakaway that day, and there usually is, then a small group of one or two, or even half-a-dozen riders will speed through ahead of the main peloton, accompanied by great cheering.

The whereabouts and the names of the riders are constantly being fed to the spectators by loudspeakers so that we know who's who, even though the information is being given in high speed excitable French.

Then, the big moment, the peloton appears and there is a whir and a blur as nearly 200 tanned and super fit riders blast past you at speeds of 30 miles an hour and above and within seconds…….they are gone. The last official cars and motor bikes make their stately progress through the town, and it dawns on you that you have been fried alive in the heat for about six hours and you saw 45 seconds of live action. Was it worth it? You bet your boots it was. Would you do it again? Yes, and tomorrow if you could. You may have even been planning to. Are you mad for doing it? Yes, slightly.

To attend a finish is a thrilling experience. I have been to quite a few, notably the Team Time Trial at Blois which I mentioned earlier when David Zabriskie's team came down *en masse* about a half mile from the finish thus ending his tenure in the yellow jersey.

Each team will cross the finishing line at intervals of about three minutes and the excitement builds as each team gets close to the day's best time or even beats it.

The finish of an ordinary stage is just as riveting. If it is a sprint stage then one needs to get into as good a viewing position as possible to watch the mayhem unfold as the world's best sprinters duke it out over the closing metres at about 40 miles an hour with the attendant high risk of crashing. I have never enjoyed watching these comings together, as I cringe at the injuries that are suffered by the riders and the tangle of those beautiful bikes (and bodies).

Probably an even greater spectacle is a mountain top finish, where the riders agonisingly claw their way to the summits, and because the speeds are slower (relatively speaking) then one can view the suffering of the riders at first hand.

1. The Author powering up Alpe d'Huez - August 2019

2. Still "powering" up the Alpe!

3. Astride the finishing Line - Alpe d'Huez conquered!

4. The Author with Sarah - Two Wolves season ticket holders after climbing l'Alpe d'Huez!

NATIONAL CYCLING PROFICIENCY

CERTIFICATE

Awarded To

BRIAN JONES

who has been trained to cycle safely and passed
the NATIONAL CYCLING PROFICIENCY TEST as
approved by the Minister of Transport, the
Secretary of State for Scotland and the Minister
of Home Affairs, Northern Ireland.

Certificate No.   2439.3

Date   23.5.63

President
The Royal Society for the Prevention of Accidents

5.Cycling Proficiency 1963

6. An early Time Trial, circa 20019, in the colours of Ogmore Valley Wheelers, still carrying big weightload

7. (Top) Astride the summit of le Mont Ventoux 2010

(Below) Moment of Triumph – the summit of Mont Ventoux

8. On the track Halesowen Cycling Club, circa 2014

9. On the boards at Newport Velodrome – Proud to be Purple in the colours of Halesowen Cycling Club circa 2013

10. Time Trialling through the grounds of Blenheim Palace circa 2014

Slimmer Brian now a personal trainer at 64

Report by Lee Watton
lee.watton@expressandstar.co.uk

A SPORTING fanatic who shed the pounds after swapping his shirt and tie for a cycling jersey plans to share his success by becoming a personal trainer at the age of 64.

Brian Jones has been sporty all his life, but started to gain weight in his 50s, eventually hitting more than 22 stone.

But the father-of-two, an independent financial adviser, decided to take on his bulge by taking up cycling at the age of 57.

Seven years on, he has cycled more than 38,000 miles and is a member of Halesowen Cycling Club competing in time trials.

Championships

He also rides in the UCI World Masters Championships in Manchester and the LVRC Veterans' Track Championships in Newport.

Thanks to the exercise and a healthy diet, Brian lost more than nine stone and is now 13 and dress quarter stone.

Brian now plans to share his success with others after qualifying to become a personal trainer. He is based at Fitness First, Olton, Solihull, and is planning to launch and lead a cycling section.

"I must be one of the oldest people to qualify for such a position as this and I am delighted to have secured a position so soon after completing my training," said Brian, of Harborne Road, Oldbury.

"I have always been an active sportsman. I played cricket to a high level in the Birmingham League and as a teenager was on the books at both Walsall and Shrewsbury football clubs."

Return to slender – Brian Jones is now a top racing cyclist

Overweight – Brian at his daughter Tamsin's graduation

"However, when I got into my 50s I started to balloon and that was when I decided to start cycling. It is a fantastic feeling to have shed so much weight and to continue to be so active."

Brian works to a strict calorie count of 2,000 calories a day – although his training regime does allow him to go over that.

"I cycle 50 miles every day. So if I eat 2,000 calories it is very likely that I will burn all of that off and more when I am on the bike. If I know, not going on a long ride I sometimes allow myself 3,000 calories because I know I can burn off as much as 3,500 calories."

Brian, who worked for Barclays Bank for 25 years and was an independent financial adviser for 20 years, said he did not want to simply retire, so he decided to pursue his passion for fitness and become a personal trainer. Brian qualified last week and has already secured the position with Fitness First.

"It is a shame that I didn't get into my chosen career. If I had taken it up when I was a teenager I don't know what I would have achieved," he said.

12. At the moment this photo was taken I was World Champion (for two minutes!)

I watched an uphill finish in Brittany which turned into a slower sprint finish as these superhuman riders sped to the line. That day the legendary Spaniard Alexandro Valverde triumphed, and I felt privileged to have seen it.

And then there is the last day on the Champs Elysees. Paris comes to a complete stop on this fabulous day as le Tour hits town, and the environs around this world-famous landmark are teeming with the hundreds of thousands of excited fans congregating to watch the spectacle.

The riders process on to the Champs Elysees in a ceremonial fashion usually paying tribute to any stalwarts who are riding their last Tour, allowing them to lead the peloton on to the boulevard and soak up the adulation of their adoring fans. This is the first of nine circuits of central Paris and as they hit the Champs for the second time the racing for that day begins in earnest.

There will probably be a doomed breakaway which is just a final opportunity for a team to showcase their sponsors one last time in front of the television cameras. Then, as the final lap unfolds, there is a brilliant scramble by the lead-out trains of the top sprinters to position themselves as beneficially as possible for their designated sprinter to try and win the sprint, which is the blue riband of stage race sprinting.

Then it is all over, this 3-week extravaganza and after the presentation of the jerseys to the winners of the different categories the teams will do a lap of honour of both sides of the boulevard. Tradition has it that a rider has to complete the 3-week race to take part in this lap, and the fans love it. I recommend this final day to all of you if you haven't experienced it. The only problem then are the withdrawal symptoms as one realises that there will be no more Tour de France for the next 49 weeks.

What has saddened me over the years are the scandals surrounding the drugs cheats who have besmirched the good name of this greatest of all sporting tests.

It is one of the biggest mysteries as to why we revere the name of the late Tommy Simpson, yellow jersey wearer and BBC Sports Personality of the Year in 1965, when he died on the Mont Ventoux in 1967 after severely dehydrating in the suffocating heat having imbibed a concoction of barbiturates and alcohol.

I am as guilty, if that is the right word, as anyone, in allowing Tom to be a such an historic hero when he committed what to me is the biggest sin in professional cycling – doping. I wish he hadn't, then he might still be with us today and who knows what else he might have achieved in what was turning out to be a great career. That last sentiment is too simplistic to be of any real value in this discussion, but it comes from the heart of a rider who follows the professional sport, whilst himself riding cleanly in amateur events.

It is no real defence to say that they all did it. I won't hear of that, and I just wish there were tests to prove, even in retrospect, who rode cleanly and who didn't, then we wouldn't have the farcical situation of Lance Armstrong's seven Maillot Jaunes being expunged from the records. For Armstrong, read Floyd Landis, and Marco Pantani and so on, and so on. This bloody list is endless and I repeat, it saddens me.

As the years have rolled by the UCI, the sport's governing body, have made numerous attempts to clean up the sport and I for one, hope they succeed. They have enlisted the services of WADA, the World Anti-Doping Association, and many, too many, professional cyclists have been outed, shamed and banned because of WADA's findings.

I am in full agreement with the blanket ban from the Olympic Games given to Russian competitors for that country's systematic use of drugs across the board with their elite athletes. We all remember East Germany, *n'est-ce pas*?

Another one of my cycling heroes, Alberto Contador, was stripped of one of his Grand Tour titles after he was found to have tested positive for a banned substance, which he blamed on contaminated meat. I don't know, but the excuses, or damned lies, that they spout after being found guilty do nothing to enhance their own cases. It remains a huge question mark to me that the climbing skills of Contador, the way he danced up mountainsides standing up on his pedals, may well have been drug fuelled. I hope not, I sincerely hope not, but it has to be doubted, doesn't it? And yes, I repeat, it saddens me.

I know that the underlying reason that pro-cyclists dope is to protect their livelihoods, because good performances lead to new and hopefully better contracts in what is, like most sports, a short career. But I am old-fashioned enough to adopt a zero-tolerance attitude towards anyone found guilty of this breach of the rules.

I won't go off on another one, but for example, I want diving by footballers eradicated. Not much to ask is it? I want honesty in sport. I fear I may not live long enough to see it, because we could well have already passed the point of no return.

CHAPTER NINE

Cycling with the Immortals

I have had the great fortune and thrill of attempting and succeeding to ride two of the Tour de France's legendary mountains, Mont Ventoux and Alpe d'Huez.

I rode up the former at the age of 59 in 2010, and the latter aged 68 in 2019. The climb up Alpe d'Huez must rank as my greatest achievement on a bicycle for a number of reasons, which I will examine later in this chapter. But let me take each mountain individually and relate my story for each of them.

My first sighting and acquaintance with the Giant of Provence, le Mont Ventoux was around the year 1991 on a family holiday to that most beautiful of areas in the South of France. This, of course, was in my non-cycling days and I was carting around the area some serious avoirdupois. My 18-year-old son however was riding quite seriously at the time, and we took his road bike to Provence for the trip.

During the holiday we drove the car up the mountain on a number of occasions, and he announced that he would like to try riding up it. With my support following him in the car he managed it as well, and he stood proudly at the summit with his bike after what I would term a wonderful achievement for one so young.

As we followed him up the mountain, we stopped to pay homage to Tommy Simpson where the memorial marks the spot of his demise during the 1967 Tour and I vowed that I would return to that very spot with a piece of cycling memorabilia which is *de rigueur*.

Tommy's last words were reputed to be "Put me back on my bike", as his severely dehydrated and drug-ravaged body was about to give out on him.

That place is only a couple of kilometres or so from the summit, but it is in the notorious treeless, arid area where so many riders have struggled, particularly when the thermometer is still in the high thirties even at that altitude. So much so that there is another memorial about a hundred metres past Tommy's spot, which marks the final resting place of an amateur Belgian cyclist.

When I became a cyclist, I vowed to myself that I would conquer *le geant de Provence* by my 60th birthday. And so in 2010, I found myself nervously at its foot in the picturesque Provencal village of Bedoin, the traditional starting point for all ascents of Ventoux by amateurs and professionals alike.

From the village it is 22 kilometres, or 14 miles in real money to its summit. It is advisable to try and avoid the unforgiving temperatures of midday and the early afternoon, so I was primed and ready to go at about 9 a.m. I intended to use the next couple of hours to achieve my ambition and stand proudly at its summit. The breakfast time temperature hovered around 26° centigrade (can anyone explain why some say celsius when they are one and the same thing, please?) with a promise of another boiling hot day to come.

The early kilometres out of Bedoin are a very gentle upward slope which hold no inkling of the terror to come, but after five or six kilometres the gradient starts to increase more noticeably, and you know you are climbing for real when the openness of the terrain becomes more forested.

One's mind needs to be occupied, and for some distance at this point the road surfaces are awash with the still visible names of the elite riders who have passed through here, names like Pantani, *Il Pirato*, who raced up these very slopes in the early nineties to set a record time.

Unfortunately his legacy was permanently tainted when he died a drug-fuelled death at a ridiculously early age, and besmirched all of his achievements by virtue of his illegal drug intake. But his image, the bandana, the goatee beard, the pirate's look, meant that he stays lodged in our minds.

On any given day there are hundreds, if not thousands of riders going up the Windy Mountain, for that is the literal translation of Mont Ventoux, and as you labour harder and harder up the ascent one tends to lock wheels with someone else who is sharing your suffering.

One such acquaintance was a German guy, probably in his forties, who spoke perfect English; which was a good job, as he probably wouldn't have been interested in my ordering meat, potatoes and peas, which is about all I can muster confidently in his mother tongue!

He told me that he was ascending the Ventoux with his 14-year-old son, who was about 100 metres ahead of us. I enquired as to how long his son had been riding and I nearly fell off my bike when my German co-pedaller said "Five weeks". That put me firmly in my place. The kid looked a complete natural. I can only assume he hadn't had time to ride a bike before now because he had been busy walking on the Moon, or climbing Mount Everest, or something!

I haven't mentioned my own training for this momentous ascent, simply because I hadn't done anything out of the ordinary, other than rack up my usual average 1,000 miles a month, but this certainly meant that I was feeling the pace, such as it was, and the pain, which was huge.

Therefore I decided to take a rain check (Ha! Rain would have been a blessed relief on this day of all days, as the mercury in the thermometer was heading north at a brisk rate) at Chalet Reynard, the café / restaurant which is a ski station in the winter months as Mont Ventoux becomes a ski resort.

Pausing for a much-needed drink and a little solid refreshment, I was amazed to find a bloke on a unicycle following me into the car park. Without dismounting he received a drink, courtesy of the café proprietor, and carried on posing for photographs for the hundreds of tourists who were in attendance.

And without breaking pedal stroke he then rode off, where I saw him later at the summit, and he was still seated on his unicycle. This was a feat which beggars belief, so "Chapeau!" to him! I later found on YouTube footage of someone who had reached the summit on a recumbent bike. Tsk! There's always someone out there to outdo you, isn't there?

Anyway, the gradient climbs seriously from Chalet Reynard, which coupled with the lunar landscape by virtue of its complete absence of trees, means that you are fully committed to reaching the summit as there is now no hiding place. On and on you press, past the Simpson memorial, where the summit buildings you can see seem so close you can touch them, but in fact there is another two to three kilometres of the steepest climbing to conquer. Then, suddenly, when your legs are screaming "No more, for God's sake!" you are on the final hairpin bend, and the 100 or so metres to the finishing line, the crossing of which gave me one hell of a thrill. I had done it!

I held my bike above my head for the obligatory photographs. Then I purchased my souvenir bandana and cycling jersey, and also a medal on a ribbon and a certificate to confirm to the world that I had reached the summit. The pictures reveal me resplendent in my Oggies kit; so chaps, another Oggie had conquered this great lump of rock. Oh, and the temperature, even at 7,000 feet on that July day was approaching 35°, or whatever measurement you care to use. It was still searingly hot.

Needless to say my total riding time was pretty damned ordinary, but I don't care. I have been more than an interested spectator in the succeeding years as my television screen has shown me pictures of epic struggles in the Tour, such as the one where Froome and

Wiggins battled their way to the summit in the year of the latter's glorious GC win, despite the feeling that Froome was the better climber, a fact that has been upheld in recent years.

I had been there and done it. I should add that the descent, which is done at breakneck speed, saw me wear through a set of brake blocks as the smell of burning rubber from them seemed to accompany my downward trajectory, and my wrists ached like hell because my grip was tight on the brake levers all the way down.

A wonderful, never to be forgotten experience, and again one is in awe of the professionals as they seem to ascend Mont Ventoux with only the smallest of inconvenience.

Alpe d'Huez was a different climb altogether. This Alp is one of a number of famous climbs in that region of the Alps where France meets Italy, but it is probably the most iconic of all the Tour de France mountain top finishes, by virtue of its 21 hairpin bends which are shown so graphically on the pictures beamed into our living rooms by that wonderful broadcast coverage of the race.

The most famous hairpin is nicknamed Dutch Corner, some two-thirds of the way up the 8-mile climb, and here there is a heaving mass of orange-shirted Dutch men and women who await with drink-fuelled raucousness the arrival of the Dutch riders. One can't claim or retain a spot on Dutch Corner if you are not wearing an orange shirt, or you are of any other nationality. This hairpin bend alone makes Alpe d'Huez unique in Tour de France folklore.

This time, unlike my climb of Mont Ventoux nine years previously, I planned and trained assiduously for it. During my time as a member of the Warwickshire Road Club there was, Bluetakked to the wall (other chewing gum-like wall sticking materials are available, I think) a poster of an aerial shot of the Alpe d'Huez, with all 21 hairpin bends named. The names commemorate previous winners of the stage from the Tour, so every bend carries a legendary title.

I was completely seduced by this poster, and subconsciously vowed to myself that this Alp must be conquered by me before I become too old to attempt it, and because I couldn't live off my Mont Ventoux laurels forever. Not that any laurels grew on the upper slopes of the Windy Mountain, because there was only sandy-coloured scree out of which nothing grows!

I was now living in Surrey, only eight miles from the foot of Box Hill, our own UK mini-version of the Alpe d'Huez, with its three hairpin bends helping you up its 1.6 mile length. I was, as always race fit, but I have never been able to climb for toffee, grunting and groaning my way at snail's pace up anything that bore even a slightly challenging gradient.

To even think about successfully ascending Alpe d'Huez, I therefore needed to slim down to a weight that would enable me to climb competitively, so something had to change. In the winter of 2017-18, as I struggled to recover from my broken wrist, I had put back on some three of the nine stone I had lost since I became a cyclist. This was understandable, as my pedalling had been restricted first by my injuries, meaning a lack of racing; and secondly, by the lousy midwinter weather keeping me off the road and forcing me on to the rollers in the kitchen, with of course, no gradient available on which to train for climbing.

So on Valentine's Day, which, coincidentally was also Shrove Tuesday in 2018, I bought a new road bike from the local Decathlon (other bike stores, blah blah blah!). I ensured it had a "granny", or third ring on the bottom bracket because, with the following day being the first day of Lent, I was going to give up biscuits, sweets, crisps and chocolates and start climbing.

In my role as a Bikeability trainer I find all the time that kids can't ride up even the slightest gradients, so I always tell them that the best way to get better at riding up hills is....... to ride up hills. Believe me, I am correct in this assertion, so I followed my own dictum.

Lent began with me showing renewed vigour and resolution, as I was still a couple of months from being able to resume time trialling following my racing accident, so my fitness needed to improve. I decided therefore to ride the eight miles to Box Hill, and promptly rode straight past it! I only realised my error after I noticed the signs to Box Hill had ceased and I was heading in the direction of Epsom, as the gradually decreasing mileage towards that town revealed.

I retraced my steps, and gave up on my laudable plans to climb the hill that day and decided to head for home. Then I accidentally stumbled upon the sign for Box Hill, which presumably after some altercation with a car, was now pointing in the wrong direction, towards Epsom! So having rewritten my plans, I now had my bearings and I was back at the foot again a day or so later.

Box Hill is to the UK as the Alpe d'Huez is to the French Alps, that is to say it is probably our most iconic climb. It was the centrepiece of the 2012 London Olympic road races, which saw the men do nine ascents and the women two before heading off back to the Mall via Richmond Park for their historic finishes.

I gritted my teeth and turned into Box Hill to begin the uphill trajectory. Because of the Olympics, Box Hill is blessed with the smoothest of black road metalled surfaces and it is the greatest of pleasures to ride, even though it is uphill.

On this first ascent I learnt that the steepest gradient is that leading to the first hairpin, but I huffed and puffed and got there, and continued upwards. The second hairpin loomed large ahead and I realised that I was making good progress, and the final hairpin presented itself, about a quarter of a mile from the National Trust café which marks the top, and there it was, done. I was a little tired, but not totally out of puff, and I was extremely pleased with myself.

I continued in this vein with more ascents over the next few days and weeks, and then one day after reaching the top, I hurtled back down to the bottom, turned round and went back up again.

Now this, in my book, represented a serious bloc of training, and a step up in intensity, and as I was now back racing, my fitness was improving all the time. Very soon I had lost the three stone that nature had wrapped around me as a punishment (or was it an incentive to become re-motivated and back in the groove?) for my accident.

I began to get serious with Box Hill, and I upped the ante not inconsiderably by doing as many as six ascents non-stop, one after the other. I was actually quite impressed with my new found ability to climb serious hills, and even though Box Hill is not, as many cyclists fear it is, the steepest hill around, it is nevertheless a rhythm climb so once on its slopes, you simply tap out a regular cadence and keep the pedals turning.

So, just as I had done many years ago when I ran the Wolverhampton Marathon for charity, I hit on the idea of climbing Box Hill 20 times in one day and offered my charitable services for the benefit of my village Choral Society, which I grace (or hinder, with my dulcet bass tones!).

I calculated that I could do this in the small number of daylight hours available at the end of November. So, backed by sponsorship running into hundreds of pounds, I was there once again at the foot of Box Hill at 8 a.m. on Saturday, 17th November 2018, supported by my other half, who was there to ply me with food and drink and rescue me by car if I had any mechanical difficulties.

There is a sport called Everesting which involves climbing anything repeatedly until the combined footage ascended reaches the 29,000 feet equivalent to the summit of Mount Everest, the world's biggest hill (!). I had read on the internet that two guys had ascended the 574-foot height gain of Box Hill some 50-odd times in one midsummer day to achieve their Everesting goal, so I reasoned that 20 times in one midwinter day was achievable.

So off I set. The plan was to do on average three ascents and descents an hour and break for meals at eight and sixteen climbs, leaving the smallest number of ascents for the third and final part when I should, in theory, be at my most fatigued. The first eight climbs were ticked off in a little over three hours, nicely on schedule. It was mid-November after all said and done, the weather was grey and cool, but I was in my element climbing what I now thought of as my very own Box Hill.

Lunch was duly downed and was most welcome, and then I climbed back into the saddle and set off again. The next eight ascents surprisingly soon passed, and as I sat down for tea I realised that my excellent fitness had not presented me with any stiffness or lethargy whatsoever. The final four ascents were commenced with me doing mental calculations as to whether I could finish before darkness fell. In the event this was accomplished with ease as I would probably have had time for one more ascent before proper darkness was upon me.

The final climb was even done in a higher gear, and I fairly raced to the summit, taking my small band of supporters by surprise as they were looking the other way when I shot into view round the final corner. My Box Hill adventure raised over £900 for the Choral Society and it felt right good. I also told myself that I was now a fully-fledged climber. And in reality, I was.

At this point the prospect of climbing Alpe d'Huez became more than a germ of an idea in my head, it became a veritable obsession! I decided that I would attempt this epic climb in August 2019 which was nine months' hence. I was now climbing the local hills on a regular, almost daily basis and true to form, logging every ascent in my diary.

I actually reside even closer to Leith Hill than I do to Box Hill, being some three-and-a-half miles only from the foot of this famous local landmark, which is where the renowned composer Ralph Vaughan Williams lived and worked.

It should be said that Leith Hill is a stiffer climb than Box Hill, albeit shorter in length at one mile; and is not such a rhythm climb, as it ramps up quite nastily in a couple of places. The road surface is also diabolical, and as it is mostly forested it can get very dark on the way up there, even on the sunniest of days. But I set about using Leith Hill as my staple climb, and would try and go up it every afternoon after work before the daylight disappeared.

No way would you contemplate coming back down this local monster in the dark, as it wouldn't be too long before you hit a pothole and somersaulted over the handlebars. But I soon came to know this unpleasant hill quite intimately, and as my climbing legs improved, then I would go up it more and more in one visit, and my record was eight successive ascents one Saturday morning. Very soon I had done more Leiths than Boxes, as I clocked up a hundred successful assaults of each.

Other local Surrey hills received periodic visits from me, and by the time I sat at the foot of Alpe d'Huez on August 5th, 2019 I was primed, ready, cycling fit and as apprehensive as hell at the prospect of what lay before me.

At lunchtime on the day before my ascent I had ridden up the first three hairpin bends (to familiarise myself with this local legend), which incidentally have the fiercest gradients, in heat which exceeded 40° Celsius. I found the intensity of the heat stifling, and I reasoned that to attempt this massive ascent in such temperatures was tantamount to cycling madness.

As this region of France was in the grip of a record heatwave despite its altitude, I couldn't expect there to be any let-up in the readings of the thermometer. But I hadn't gone all that way to be dissuaded from riding by the sunshine, so the following morning immediately after eating my condemned man's hearty breakfast at 8.30 a.m. I set off from my hotel, which was about a mile and a half from the start of the climb.

I was reckoning on the upward "dash" taking me about two hours, so I should be breasting the tape at about 10.30, before you could actually fry eggs on the pavement.

The ride to the start from my hotel village of Bourg d'Oisans is refreshingly pan-flat, so I started pedalling in order to turn my legs over to get those crucial limbs warmed up sufficiently. I turned right at the first roundabout then left at the second, and that was it, we were on, as the road started to rise.

You begin to feel the gradient in your legs straight away, which is probably a nervous reaction to what is in store, and after what seemed like an eternity but was in fact half a mile, you reach the first hairpin bend.

As you go round it you try to resist thinking to yourself "One down, 20 to go", but you do think exactly that, you can't help it. You pedal through the second and third hairpins which are equally as challenging as the first, and then some relief appears as the gradient lessens a little and the bends start to come along more frequently.

It is always advisable to keep your brain occupied on rides such as this, and I employed the use of trivia to keep my mind away from the task in hand. Things like – what was the best thing before sliced bread, or why does it always rain at the end of a dry spell? You get the picture. This worked, because when I re-focussed suddenly, I had consigned eight or nine bends to history.

You look at the names of the stage winners on each road sign at the hairpins, and if you are familiar with them then you imagine that you are indeed following in the tyre tracks of these immortals.

Then, as the punishing sun started to increase its intensity and I reached the halfway point, I did a quick state-of-the-ride check on my progress, and found that I was in fact going surprisingly well, with minimal fatigue in my legs and the mental willpower to continue the upward push.

The mountain was full of riders attempting the ride and I may have overtaken one or two, but certainly big numbers of younger and fitter cyclists were going past me, but not without a cheery "Hi", or "Bon jour", or "Guten Tag". (Sorry, I don't know any more languages!).

Another quick time-consuming calculation and I realised that there must be several hundred, or even a four-figure number of cyclists going up this particular Alpe on any one day, and this was a Monday, not even a weekend day!

Yet another hairpin and all of a sudden, with about six bends to go, I was at Dutch Corner! The thrilling atmosphere and the teeming, orange-clad hordes of alcohol-soaked Dutchmen that beautify the Tour de France were, of course, nowhere to be seen on this day, so I just had to imagine the goings-on over the years at this iconic spot. But at least I can say I have ridden through there, and then it was onwards and upwards for what was beginning to take shape as the final push. With hairpin bend number 18 successfully negotiated the most wonderful coincidence then occurred.

I was climbing Alpe d'Huez wearing my brand-new skinsuit, the design of which I had done myself, with my able assistant, my Directrice Sportive Liz, earlier in the summer. Its main feature was that it was in the colours of our beloved football team Wolverhampton Wanderers, which are, of course, their world-renowned old gold and black.

The bodice was old gold, and the collar and cuffs and a fancy pattern on the chest were black. Not to mention a black circle in the central groin area, which the makers threw in mischievously. On the back I had added a feature which I believe might catch on in the world of cycling, my surname! Well, it has been a feature on football shirts now for ages and other sports are catching on. My name "JONES" is emblazoned on my upper back in black capital letters. Pretty damned trendy!

This all made me very visible as I pedalled ever upwards.

Gradually I was joined by an English lady who began to ride with me, and we started to engage in conversation. She introduced herself as Sarah, and when she found out I was English she enquired as to where I hailed from, as my accent was intriguing her. I told her I originated from near Birmingham, and she said she was from Wolverhampton, and what's more, I was riding in the colours of her footie team, the mighty Wolves.

I had the pleasure of telling her that I and my helper, the sainted Liz, who was following in the car behind me, were both season ticket holders at Molineux, the home of the Wolves, and Sarah said so was she! She then, being a lot younger than me pressed onwards and upwards, and said she would see us at the summit. My thoughts were then reoccupied with the last two bends of the Alp.

What a wonderful coincidence, and as no-one else got between me and her as the finishing line hove into view, then two successive finishers on the majestic Alpe d'Huez would be Wolverhampton Wanderers season ticket holders. What were the chances of that?

The end was truly in sight, and the ski resort of Alpe d'Huez now presented a welcoming sight to my eyes and the prospect of final relief to my weary but still willing legs. I crossed the line, which is permanently marked in the tarmac and has presided over the finishes of the greatest climbers in the history of cycling, let alone little old me; and I don't mind admitting there was a lump in my throat as I congratulated myself on what I had just achieved.

I love it when projects come to fruition and this one had been a labour of love for me over the previous twelve months or so. I pulled over to the side, parked the bike and then disaster struck! I couldn't swing my right leg over the saddle as my right groin muscle had completely seized up on me. It was an injury that I can only describe as a repetitive strain injury caused by being in one position for the previous hour and 50 minutes.

I didn't change position even to stand up on the pedals from time to time, having remained seated in the same position for the entire climb, and when I suddenly moved to dismount from my trusty steed, then the muscle seized up completely.

Looking back, this was a schoolboy error but this information was now firmly lodged in my databank entitled "Know Your Own Body". Occasionally one does have to learn the hard way. I had to be peeled off my bike and then found that I couldn't walk. In fact I could barely shuffle along, and had to drag my right leg, which was now quite painful, to obtain any sort of forward movement.

The bike in question was my £400 Triban 500 with a triple front chain ring, which was fully and gainfully employed throughout the whole of the day's adventure. Chapeau Triban!

I did manage to sit down in a café, and ordered a soothing drink when Sarah reappeared. She, and I, wanted photographs to record this momentous achievement, and after I had stood upright, with all the agility of a forklift truck, we were photographed for posterity. But more than that, we told her that we would send the photograph to the programme editor at the Wolves accompanied by a few words of explanation and see if we could get it into the next edition.

We calculated that the next match we would all be attending back at home would be the Europa League fixture versus Torino FC from, you guessed it, Italy. Sure enough, there it was in the match-day programme, the very first photo on the supporters' page with our story proudly set out underneath. We managed to text Sarah at Molineux on the night as she sat in the grandstand opposite to us to ensure that she had seen it; and she had.

So I conquered Alpe d'Huez. I loved it, and at the age of 68 was fit enough to make sure that I was not distressed by the climb (I am not counting the pulled muscle at the summit, because I have learned from that – note to self, one must continually change position to avoid that kind of inconvenient, and painful, repetitive strain injury).

I always enquire of myself was it worth it, and would I do it all again? The answers to those two questions are "Yes it was, and yes emphatically, I will return, Monsieur Alpe, for I have fallen in love with you and what's more I fancy a crack at your cousin, le Galibier, further along the valley. You see if I don't!".

My latest ambitious project was to ride the Leith Hill Octopus, the name given to the eight different routes to the summit of Leith Hill, and I accomplished this in March 2020, before the Coronavirus lockdown. The combined distance of this day's climbing purgatory is over 60 miles, half of which are unpleasantly uphill, the other half being madcap descents on road surfaces which will never put a spirit level to any trouble.

The day I selected was, of course, cold and wet, rendering the roads and lanes of the Octopus even more unwelcoming, but I began at about 8.30 in the morning with the long three-mile slog up to Coldharbour from Dorking. This was a prudent starting start point, as it dispensed with one of the more difficult ascents at the very beginning.

This was immediately followed by the only leg I hadn't attempted in training – Sheephurst Lane. Containing in places a single track with occasional passing places, the lane degenerated into a narrow thoroughfare with a mossy strip along its centre and one short, steep section which I encountered successfully.

Next came the difficult climb back up Henhurst Cross Lane followed by the halfway point, reached with the long but not difficult climb back up Hollow Lane.

Time for refreshment after three tiring hours in the saddle,so I paused for biccies and fruit before setting off to deal with relatively easier climbs in Broomhall Lane and Powderwood Road.

Finally, there were two legs of the Octopus remaining to conquer. First was the legendary Leith Hill itself – one and a half miles of downright nastiness, but which I had ridden 240 times in the last eighteen months. Fortified by glucose tablets I made surprisingly light work of this before sitting at the foot of the final climb.

This was Tanhurst Lane - the steepest leg of the Octopus, and a veritable sting in the tale. I had saved one last energy gel for this *bete noir* and I remained seated on my trusty bike as I gulped it nervously down.

I decided to attack this final ascent positively, and I watched my computer tick down each one hundredth of the mile to the summit, and then suddenly…..

I was there! The Octopus done and dusted. Total riding time – five and a half hours. Another challenge accomplished. Feeling, as always, proud of myself I had enough energy (remarkably) to belt home, where I slobbed around in a lovely warm bath with a welcome cup of Bovril.

Next up? It has to be Lands End to John O'Groats – LEJOG – and on a lesser scale I must do a charity ride from London to Paris when I can fit it in, Covid-19 allowing. I would also love to ride the length of France from Calais to Nice – now that would be a ride to savour. There is much more of my dotage to misspend yet. Watch this space!

CHAPTER TEN

Further Afield

Whilst clocking up my first 138,000 miles (and counting) I have turned the pedals in some very interesting places. When I am not actually in the saddle I tend to read every book about cycling, and especially le Tour de France, that I can lay my cycling-mitted hands on.

However, the best book that I have read on cycling was written by David Byrne, the lead singer of the American rock band Talking Heads. This particular band have a curious place in my heart because their bass guitarist, a lady named Tina Weymouth, is the only person I have ever been able to find who was born on the same day as me, the 22nd of November 1950. I digress (Get on with it! I hear you cry!).

David Byrne tours the world with the band, but his real passion is riding a bike. This book, which I so loved reading, is an actual travelogue of all the places where he has ridden. His modus operandi is that whenever he touches down at a Talking Heads tour venue, the most important thing he does is to hire a road bike, and every free moment he has he is out and about on it.

Byrne then wrote, in glorious detail in this book, about what he sees in the various places, the state of the roads, the varied geography and architecture, and the reaction of the local traffic to him, a mere bloke on a road bike. I found this view on cycling utterly absorbing as he took us to, I recall, places in every continent. Read it, and you are accompanying him, say, to Sydney, Australia, or Singapore, Moscow, Stockholm, London, Rio de Janeiro, and Cape Town to name but a few.

His band are always known by its biggest hit 'Same as it Ever Was' which is a great song, but to me David Byrne is also a cycling hero. I wish I had written that book.

Other celebrity cyclists who have caught my attention are the fabulously rich Lord Alan Sugar, who apparently owns seven Pinarello road bikes, one for every day of the week, and when once asked why he rides a different Pinarello every day of the week, he quite properly answered "Because I can"! Was that one of the daftest questions ever asked?

Gary Kemp, lead guitarist of the British rock band Spandau Ballet, and one of the brothers Kemp who portrayed the Kray Twins in a renowned film, is another cycling hero of mine, as apparently he meets a group of mates every day when he is available and they go on a training ride around Hyde Park in London.

Lee Dixon, the famous football pundit who turned out with great distinction for many seasons with Arsenal and England, has also fallen in love with the bike since his football days were over and I respect him hugely for that.

But back to where the bike has taken me, and whilst I am not about to launch into a David Byrne-esque travelogue, where have I been? Dealing with the UK first of all, I have ridden races in all of the counties inclusively, ranging from Cornwall in the South as far north as Lancashire in the north west of England to Northumberland in the north east. I think the only counties missing from that list are Kent (and I live within 20 miles of the county), Norfolk and Suffolk.

In Wales I have raced across most of the south of the principality, and have also set off on lone as well as organised rides taking in the mountains of Wales. I have ridden across the coastal roads of North Wales as well.

I have not ridden or trained north of Liverpool on the western wing of the country, but when my daughter lived and worked in that city I rode one Saturday morning from her home in South Liverpool, in

Aigburth, due north across the city centre from where I pedalled around the home of the Grand National, Aintree racecourse, (on a bike let me add), and then headed back south towards Stanley Park, the site of the two football clubs, Liverpool and Everton.

Reaching Goodison Park, Everton's ground, first, I was able to have a look around, since there was a little activity going on as their box office was selling tickets for their match the following day, the Sunday. With their welcoming friendliness putting a spring into my pedals, I cycled across Stanley Park the half mile or so to Anfield, celebrated ground of Liverpool FC. I rode through the world-famous Shankly Gates, only to be greeted, if that is the correct word, by a jobsworth, who enquired as what I thought I was doing. "Just having a look around" I said in my Everton-inspired jovial mood. "Well, clear off. We're closed!" was his terse response, and I thought to myself that there was a contrast in the way the two clubs greet casual visitors. Let's hear it for PR. Everton don't do much for me anyway, but I can't spare the time of day for Liverpool after that unsavoury episode.

After I had been riding for twelve months I embarked on my biggest cycling challenge yet, when I decided to adventurously spend a weekend cycling from Cardiff to London to watch the final stage of the 2008 Tour of Britain take place along the Thames Embankment in London. This was done on a whim, as I only arranged it all in the week leading up to my departure on the Friday evening in early September.

Putting together an itinerary, I trawled the internet and booked three overnight stops in small hotels or bed and breakfast establishments. Everything fell into place and I left home at about 4 p.m. on Friday afternoon, and set out to ride to my first resting place across the Severn estuary, in the lovely small town of Chipping Sodbury, in South Gloucestershire.

This first watering hole was timed so that I would reach the hotel as the daylight faded, but that first ride was thrown into jeopardy when I suffered the cyclist's worst nightmare, a puncture in my rear wheel. As I was only a couple of miles from Sodding Chipbury, as it had now become, I elected to walk the final distance. On reaching the hotel and enquiring whether there was a bike shop in the locality, the hotel proprietor informed me that there was, and furthermore it was only a couple of hundred yards or so from the hotel.

So as to husband my resources, I asked the bike shop to put me a new inner tube in, and regaled him with what I was attempting in this great cycling adventure. He seemed only too happy to help, and he got me going at about 9 a.m. on that Saturday morning and so off I pedalled on the long road to London.

The ride was just over a hundred miles and it was a none too difficult ride, mostly along the A4 in the Thames Valley with no serious hills to hinder my onward progress. Through Chippenham, Marlborough, Hungerford, Newbury, Reading and Maidenhead I plundered, and hit West London close to teatime where I found the bed and breakfast room I had booked in Ealing. This was a most enjoyable day in the saddle, blessed as it was by clement weather and I settled down to a most welcome meal in a local public house, which I devoured heartily before turning in tired but satisfied.

The following morning, Sunday, involved a short 10-mile ride to the Embankment where I took up a vantage point near the finishing line of the Tour, and watched spellbound as the peloton hurtled past several times before the final sprint brought the week-long event to a thrilling climax. I even saw myself in full glorious Technicolor on the televised highlights programme, which I watched and repeatedly paused in the appropriate place when I got home!

After the cycling finished I then headed back out of London to begin the return journey.

I rode about 30 miles to Reading, where my final stop had been booked, and here I was allowed to take my bike to bed with me. Well, not quite; but the hotel kindly allowed me to have my trusty steed in my hotel room out of harm's way.

The final day, Monday, saw me ride from Reading to Cardiff, again over 100 miles, and I managed to add some unnecessary distance by taking a wrong turn near Bath, and having to retrace my steps to get back onto the pre-ordained path. Nevertheless, this was the conclusion to a most exciting adventure, and I totally recommend this type of weekend's riding to anyone who wants to stretch themselves by riding not exactly out of one's comfort zone, but certainly riding into the unknown. It was enormous fun.

The mountains of South Wales are a challenge. There is the Bwlch, just inland from the sea, which is a long and winding road (is there a song in there somewhere?) and is an unremitting climb, in whichever direction you tackle it.

I once did a mountain time trial on the Bwlch to earn a solitary point for my club, the Ogmore Valley Wheelers, in its successful quest to win the coveted annual Magic Dragon series for clubs in the area. This climb took place one spring Sunday morning, and we assembled at the foot of the Bwlch where I had inadvisably based myself and parked my car for after the race.

I slogged my way up the mountain in a skinsuit and little else, cresting the summit where the finish line awaited the riders on a flat section; which, incidentally, had magnificent views. But not today. When we reached the finish a freezing mist was waiting to greet us, and when I started what should have been a joyous descent back to my waiting car, I nearly died of hypothermia as the freezing mist, together with a savage drop in temperature and the wind chill of the descent, meant that my scantily-clad flesh was blue when my shivering hands reached the car. Note to self – next time, park the car at the top of the mountain and cycle down to the start. Not rocket science, is it?

I have ridden a few Audax events in this area and the circumstance of one or two them need recounting. An Audax is an internationally-devised event (The word Audax originated from France, and I believe the governing body of this type of ride is administered from that country), and is designed for long-distance endurance riders. It is not a race, simply one has to ride from A to B, usually over a distance of 200 kilometres (approximately 125 miles). One can devise one's own route, but you have to report to three pre-arranged checkpoints, usually a café where the grateful proprietor in return for your custom will stamp your *brevet* (your race card), which proves you have been there.

The Audax events leave the start point at, say 7.30 a.m., and you are allocated 14 hours to complete the ride. I was once involved in a Saturday Audax ride through mid-Wales, and the mini-peloton I was briefly with came upon the pre-arranged café stop in some one-horse town at about 4 p.m., only to find the particular establishment had closed for the day. Oh, calamity! As we all needed our brevets validating. (No, that isn't a euphemism!).

Quick as a flash, and I wish I could think on my feet like this, someone had the bright idea of getting a printed balance statement from the bank ATM across the road which would have the date, time and venue on it. Job done, as these chitties were accepted back at HQ, even if the race organiser did find out how much we all had currently in our bank accounts!

I once made stately progress in an Audax which started at Tewkesbury in Gloucestershire in the merry month of December with its short daylight hours and freezing temperatures, and stopped for lunch at the lovely teashop opposite Ludlow Castle, in the south of Shropshire. After my brevet was duly stamped, I set off with my great cycling mate Mike (more of whom anon,) and we left Ludlow via a Bwlch-like climb as we headed towards the Welsh border in the direction of Kington. This used to be in the county of Radnorshire, before that name disappeared in those pointless re-drawings and re-namings of the county boundaries.

126

Having reached the summit of this unexpected climb with more than a few grunts and groans because I don't like surprise mountain climbs, I prefer to be forewarned, and had just started to settle into a relaxing cadence when – my right pedal fell off! The crank had sheared away from the bottom bracket without so much as a by-your-leave (whatever that phrase means), and I was sat there, at least 50 miles from my car and with a bike possessing one pedal. I told Mike to go on, as the smell of burning martyr pervaded the air, because, like a good mate, he said he would stay with me until help arrived. He had to be forcibly put back on his bike, as I didn't want my misfortune to spoil his endeavours.

I didn't quite know what to do, so I turned around and reasoned that as we had just climbed for three miles out of Ludlow, then retracing my steps would mean I could freewheel back into the town on my one remaining pedal, and find a bike shop and thus procure a repair job. I raced back down the mountain and re-entered Ludlow, and enquired where the bike shop might be, if indeed one existed.

I was directed into a side street to shop premises which bore some resemblance to Arkwright's store in the TV comedy "Open All Hours". The aged proprietor appeared to confirm that my pedal had indeed fallen off, which wasn't exactly earth-shattering news as I had just put the broken component into his hand.

"Right" he said. "I'm very busy at the moment, and we are closing in about an hour and don't open on Sundays (tomorrow), so the earliest I can fix this up for you is Monday morning. Leave me your name and contact number and I will call you when it's fixed", he (un)helpfully suggested.

At this point I felt it opportune to appraise him of my circumstances, that I was 50 miles from my car, and I needed to be back there tonight, preferably, and most definitely accompanied by my bike. I couldn't imagine how many train journeys it would take for me to criss-cross my way across the countryside back to Tewkesbury, or even if that was achievable on a Saturday night.

And the prospect of a taxi ride from Ludlow to base camp would probably cost more than my bike was worth.

So I threw the ball back into his court, and told him I would love him forever if he could fix it that very afternoon, and send me on my way. Without pausing for thought he said "Oh, right-o", and promptly reattached the pedal crank to my bottom bracket with that latent skill cycle mechanics seem to possess! The old chap must have been on a promise before he hastily rearranged his repair priorities!

With a newly patched-up machine I set off for back the way I had travelled towards Tewkesbury during the morning session mid- to late afternoon. By the time I reached the city of Worcester darkness had fallen by 4.30 pm (it was mid-December, lest ye forget), but I was now only about 10 or 12 miles from Tewkesbury along the famous A38, one of the longest and most celebrated A roads in the whole country.

I left Worcester's city boundary and pedalled off towards my final destination. It needs putting on the table right now that the A38 between these two old places has not been blessed with street lighting. And traffic had become very sparse as the evening hours were ticking by.

This meant that I was frequently alone with only the weak rays provided by my totally inadequate front light, which meant that I couldn't even make out the side of the road, so I had no idea where I was riding.

As my eyes became accustomed to the lack of light I could just about make out where the side of the road was, and after about an hour of the hairiest riding conditions I have ever been involved, in I started the final descent into Tewkesbury accompanied by that wonderful invention, street lighting. Back at the HQ, after my brevet was handed in for scrutiny, although this was rendered null and void by my mishap, I gratefully and ravenously tucked into vast quantities of mashed potato, grated cheese and baked beans.

Audaxes can be very difficult rides if things go against you, but they are challenges that are fun to take on, and I wish I had done more. For me it is a winter activity because of my time trialling calendar but I will do more in the future, I have promised myself.

*

Which brings me back to the subject of my great cycling mate Mike Lane. When I was an Independent Financial Advisor working from home in Cardiff, Mike was the representative for Royal London International, an offshore investment company based in the Isle of Man, and his role was to provide the support for us advisors if we wished to recommend one of his company's products to any of our clients.

Let me say that in those days that if he had wanted to, he could have earned a very tidy living as a look-alike for Tony Blair, the erstwhile Prime Minister. The resemblance really was uncanny. He used to come to my house and after we had gone through the necessary business agenda, our conversation used to turn to, and remain on, the subject of cycling; more specifically what I was up to with regard to training and competing.

Mike, it transpired, used to ride a bike in his youth, (he is about three years younger than me) and his sporting career and expertise had led to him being, amongst other things, a tenpin bowling coach (having, he said, scored a maximum 300 frame score, equivalent to a 147 maximum break at snooker – Chapeau Mike!) and I later found out he had a racing car in his garage which was worth about £30,000. A fascinating bloke.

These conversations used to spill over into the local coffee shop as Mike's visits became more and more frequent. This was quite remarkable given that he lived across the Severn Estuary near Bristol, about 35-40 miles away.

Eventually our meetings had whetted his appetite for cycling, and he subsequently joined one of his local clubs, the Severn Road Club (SRC) and bought himself a time trialling bike. As he weighed about as much as a wet whippet, he quickly got himself up to race fitness and the next thing I knew, he was riding in the SRC Tuesday night time trials near Aust, alongside the Severn Estuary. I was easily persuaded to join him each week, and I looked forward to these races. It was a reasonably fast course and contained the hair-raising start which I have chronicled elsewhere, on which I hit my highest - ever speed on a bike, whilst frightening myself half, no, three quarters, to death. Mike even thanked me for being an inspiration to him. Oh, how those particular tables would be turned!

All went well for a time as we became best buds on the bike and I joined him occasionally in what for me, was my introduction to Audax riding, which Mike was also now getting into more and more.

Then one fateful day in high summer, his work took him to clients on the North Wales coast and he duly booked into a hotel near Rhyl. Taking the opportunity in the time his work allowed, he quickly got out onto his bike for a training ride and set off on the fast A road that runs parallel to the coastline.

When he was cycling back to his hotel from this ride, he joined a slip road to take him from a High Street back onto the dual carriageway. Moving to his right to re-join the slow lane, he was promptly wiped out by a German coach and dumped 100 or so metres up the road and left for dead on the grass verge.

The first I knew about this was when his wife phoned me and told me what had happened to him, and asked if I could get up there to the hospital in Rhyl and visit him. It was the other end of the country, and by now I was back living in Birmingham, but I hotfooted it up there as soon as I could. Walking into his hospital room there was my poor mate Mike, wired up to several contraptions, having suffered multiple fractures, with severe cuts and bruises to whatever else had not been broken in his poor body.

He seemed to have some difficulty grasping who I was but eventually it seemed to dawn on him and I was able, I think, to reassure him that I was there for him. In itself this was of no consequence whatsoever, as there was nothing I could do that would help him, other than support him by being there when he needed it.

His wife thanked me profusely for my visit, and I made her promise to keep me informed on a daily basis of Mike's condition and progress, saying that I would return as soon as possible to see him again. As I drove away, I was filled with the realisation that Mike was lucky to be alive; and also that it seemed his riding, and certainly his racing days, were over.

I did return the following week, where there was a small improvement in his level of awareness; but alarmingly, he said I was glad I had visited him as he had waited patiently to see me. He had no recollection whatsoever of my previous visit, and he proceeded verbatim to have the same conversation with me as he had on my first call. This was extremely worrying. Also, he didn't have any recall of what had befallen him in his accident. There were only eye-witness reports of the whole thing.

Eventually he made it back to his home more than 200 miles away and he began the long road to recovery. And it was indeed the longest and rockiest, metaphorically speaking, of roads, as his injuries were so severe that he had to be patient while nature took a very arduous course.

My frequent visits to him were difficult for me as now he had very little sense of recall. The bubbliest of personalities with which he had been blessed in his Tony Blair lookalike days had been replaced by dark moods, in which he would despair and chastise himself heartbreakingly for the hand Lady Luck had dealt him.

After months and months of intense and frustrating rehab he then told me that he had hitched up some contraption to winch him back onto the bike, indoors of course, so that he could work towards a return to the road.

I was astounded by this news, and whilst I was encouraging in my conversations with him, I couldn't really foresee it happening.

The changed person he had become was made all the more incredible by the fact that he had not had a haircut since the accident, and was now able to tie his hair back in a ponytail. Can you imagine Tony Blair with a ponytail? Hard to see, isn't it!

There was of course a lawsuit pending, and he also had to admit the defeat of any hopes of returning to work. His powers of concentration had been destroyed in the smash and he couldn't focus on anything for more than a few minutes at a time, he told me.

I still came down from Birmingham whenever I was able to compete in the SRC Tuesday evening time trial, and the members would enquire as to the latest state of Mike's health and what the prognosis might be. Eventually this remarkable man got himself back on his bike, and ventured outdoors for his first tentative pedal strokes.

A direct result of his horrendous crash were mental problems, easily reducing him to tears of frustration even when he was talking to you. But despite all this he managed to improve encouragingly in the saddle; and then he informed me that he was going to ride an Audax. I could barely believe my ears, but it was true. We were in the year 2011 and he was back on his bike within two years of his accident.

Incredibly, he did go on and participate in an Audax, and then he rode another, and then another.

Very soon he was riding not only at weekends but during the week as well. His lovely long-suffering wife, who had nursed him back to fitness, stood by him and allowed him to do these long-distance endurance rides. Let's face it, the alternative outcome to his state of mind after what he had been through was too difficult to contemplate.

And he still hadn't had a haircut since his accident and his tight, smart Blairite (wrong word probably!) hairstyle was now reaching down towards his backside.

If I attempted to grow my hair it wouldn't have reached my backside even if I smeared lawn fertiliser on my pate!

He rigged up a trailer to his road bike, in which his day-to-day belongings and requirements could accompany him as he set off on Audax after Audax. I never fully realised how determined a man he really was and his accident, for all the other ways it changed him, had not dimmed the fire inside his belly. Rather the opposite.

Because, I am proud to report, that in the six years 2012 to 2017 inclusive he became the Audax champion of the UK, with no-one getting near the points totals he amassed week by week throughout those six incredible years.

All of his rides are logged on his individual page of the Audax website and most of that time, the whole year round, he was riding four or five times per week, mostly in the midweeks on his own, with his trailer, and always completing the minimum of the classic Audax distance of 200 kilometres.

I would wager that you, the reader, may even have driven past him on occasion without realising the epic journey this man was engaged in. He even undertook the long distance Audax of 600 kilometres (about 375 miles) in one weekend. It was, I believe, the most astonishing series of rides ever undertaken by an Audax rider, certainly in the UK. And this was him putting two fingers up to adversity and fighting back. And how.

To me, his is the most remarkable story I can report in cycling, and although we haven't been in touch for some time now, he will forever remain the most heroic of men in my eyes.

Oh, and through all that historic and monumental run as UK Audax champion he never cut his hair, which had grown to a length any Rastafarian would be envious of! Chapeau Mike!

*

I started my personal cycling odyssey in the beautiful countryside of Brittany back in September 2007 and racked up my first couple of hundred miles in the homeland of my favourite sporting event, the Tour de France.

It struck me as I was getting into riding, how smooth the French roads are, and I wondered, do they use a different mix of tarmac to that which we slap onto our poor roads in the UK? Our highways, even allowing for what is probably a larger volume of traffic, seem to resort to potholes as soon as either the temperature drops or we have a moderately heavy downpour.

The French system of road signage is confusingly different to ours. Before you venture onto the road you have to come to terms with the vagaries and differences of the French language. This can lead to some interesting misconceptions when on Gallic territory!

Par exemple (swift and gratuitous use of the French lingo there!) it is a fact that French taps which are marked with the letter 'C' actually mean hot, or '*Chaud*', and that if you are half asleep you can easily scald yourself until you realise that 'C' doesn't mean cold, (it doesn't bear thinking about what the letter 'F' might stand for on the other taps!).

As if that wasn't bad enough, you are then confronted with the road signs and what information they are actually providing for you, Johnny Foreigner. In the UK the 'A' roads, (did we used to call them trunk roads? Although I have to confess I never saw any elephants on them!) are on signs with a green background and our motorway signs are on blue backgrounds.

One day in that first month of inexperienced cycling, I cycled through a small French town and was looking for the main road back to base. I saw the green sign and routinely cycled off down the slip road to join the dual carriageway. "Bloody hell!" I thought as I rode on, "these road surfaces get better and better. And how friendly the drivers are, especially the lorry drivers, as they toot their horns whilst they shoot past me, recognising that I am a tourist enjoying a good ride around their welcoming country!".

However, after a short while when it seemed that every single vehicle was now honking their hooters at me, then I began to think that this was a bit strange. It was at that moment that, thankfully, the reality struck me with the force of a lightning bolt. I was actually riding along a French autoroute, or motorway, having misread the signs which, in France are opposite, as previously described, to those in the UK.

In *la belle France*, it is green for the motorways, which are also 'A' roads, as A stands for *Autoroute*; and blue for their trunk roads, which are 'N' roads, or *Route National*. Once the awful truth had lodged itself between my ears and I had been made aware of the danger I had put myself in, not to mention the illegality of what I was doing, I needed to change my situation pretty damned quickly.

I bet the autoroute control cops had spilt their cappuccinos all over their closed-circuit television monitors as they looked on, open-mouthed and wide-eyed at the entertainment I was inadvertently providing!

I slammed my anchors on and got off that pesky autoroute as quickly as possible on foot, taking the only way available to me. As I was in the middle of the countryside (when aren't you in France?), I scaled a fence at the side of the road, bike and all. I found myself in a field of crops, at least a quarter of a mile trek from the nearest tarmacked stretch of ridable road, which I could just make out in the distance beyond the greenery in front of me. A salutary lesson was learnt that day, and so early on in my cycling career.

It was also during these early sorties on a bike that I first wore cleated shoes, and I couldn't quite grasp the technique of cleating into the pedals. And to make matters much worse, once I was cleated in, I was nearly spraining my ankles trying to uncleat.

This difficulty, or lack of technique, I was having with my new footwear came to a head when I had to stop at a set of traffic lights, again in France, and uncleat whilst I waited for the green light.

Easier said than done, as I unceremoniously fell over on to the side of the road in an unholy heap, much to the mirth of the French drivers who were watching in a bemused manner this silly English person providing such an hilarious and embarrassed pantomime. I had deposited myself on my back in a gorse bush in the most undignified fashion with my feet and bike sticking up in the air, still cleated in! Eventually a kind local Frenchman got out of his 2CV and helped me back to my feet. In between Gallic guffaws he kept saying *"Mon Dieu!"* Can't think why!

As well as my two (for me) epic ascents of those great mountains, Mont Ventoux and Alpe d'Huez, I have ridden quite a lot in Provence, in the South of France, both on the coast and in the hinterland. Riding along the coast is a wonderful experience.

The Cote d'Azur, the millionaire's playground that stretches about 200 miles from Marseille in the west to Monaco in the east as it nestles against the frontier with Italy, is the most beautiful of roads on which to ride. One passes through resort after resort, with the size and opulence of the yachting community on full view as any moment you expect to come face to face with James Bond in his open-topped sports car. I have had some wonderful rides, ranging from the Promenade des Anglais on the seafront at Nice to beautiful resorts such as Argeles-sur-Mer and Cagnes-sur-Mer as far as Cannes itself.

I was saddened and horrified when the terrorist attack caused such tragedy on that world-renowned road in Nice.

This road, which hugs the coastline, is known as the *Basse Corniche*, which translates roughly as the Low Highway, and there are three corniches serving the Cote d'Azur. The *Moyenne Corniche*, or Middle Highway, straddles the coast halfway up the mountain sides which grace the coastline.

Then there is the *Grande Corniche*, or Big Job, that most spectacular of routes, with its pencil-thin bridges seemingly hanging in the sky. Skirting the tops of the mountains, it then tears through tunnel after tunnel. (Once they have cleared the unimaginable wreckage left by the Bond films, as these always seem to include a car chase through them.)

Riding in the hinterland of Provence, in the shadow of *le Geant de Provence, le Mont Ventoux* as it presides over this glorious countryside, has been my pleasurable lot on a number of occasions. Summertime in this part of the world has always seemed to me to be God's earthly hint as to what awaits us in heaven.

Mont Ventoux is also nicknamed the "Bald Mountain" or the "Beast of Provence", both of which say it all really. Wherever you cycle, if you, as I have always tried to, base yourselves in the picturesque market town of Bedoin, then you can see *le Geant* wherever you are. This area is not flat, in fact it is challengingly hilly, but the effort required to traverse this countryside is dwarfed by the sheer unadulterated natural beauty upon which your eyes feast.

There are three routes to the summit of Mont Ventoux, the classic ascent, from Bedoin itself and two others; an approach from the east starting at the picturesque hillside village of Sault, which provides a longer ride but an easier gradient and which meets the Bedoin route near Chalet Reynard; or the assault from the north side, starting at the village of Malaucene, which is as difficult as coming up from Bedoin itself.

As if this vista is not aesthetically pleasing enough, then the weather in this area is incomparable. The Mediterranean climate, as we are about 80 miles from the Med itself, is regularly as warm as an oven, but always it is summer in all its finery. One day I must go back there and renew my acquaintance with that wonderful area, and especially my old and treasured friend, le Mont Ventoux.

I have ridden briefly in Germany, in its new capital city Berlin. Post-reunification, Berlin is a brilliantly vibrant city, teeming with history, and we all are aware of where this city has come from to where it stands at the present day.

I rented a hybrid bike from a cycle shop near to the Brandenburg Gate, and rode through the Tiergarten, the huge park which starts at the very Gate itself and spreads before you as far as the Olympic Stadium, that edifice built by the Nazis to showcase their ill-fated 1936 Olympiad. This has now been modernised to be a superb modern arena, which stages Grand Prix athletics events on its trademark blue track whilst doubling as the 80,000-seater home of Bundesliga football team Hertha Berlin FC.

The park in the very heart of the city seems to be a peculiarly German phenomenon and I recall a similar patch of greenery in Stuttgart, which stretches for about five miles. The main feature of life in these parks seems to be that on Sundays, the traditional day of rest, German families all assemble in the parks and picnic away the daylight hours.

I remember in the Berlin Tiergarten there is a carillon tower and every hour the air rings with its pleasant chimes. The park itself is delightfully flat, and its pathways take you along the waterside as the River Spree winds its way through the capital.

I rode out as far as the castle, the Schloss at Charlottenburg, and enjoyed a very pleasant tour around the interior of this historic and beautiful building. I know I keep saying something similar, but I would love to return to the German capital and retrace that leisurely pedal through the peaceful Tiergarten. What a delightful thing to say, hinting at peace and Berlin in the same sentence.

I rode through the heart of Austria in May 2008 on an exciting, no, it was more than that, a wonderfully exhilarating, ride along the Danube from Salzburg, via Linz, to the capital of Austria, the fabulous city of Vienna.

Collecting my bike from the hotel in Salzburg, I set off into the foothills of the Austrian Alps on an unforgettable cycling adventure. This is Sound of Music territory, and the pathways out of this beautiful town take you into the forested areas which are the prelude to actually joining the Danube at Linz, as it makes its way through the most beautiful area of Austria. What am I talking about? The whole of Austria is beautiful. Stunningly so.

I feel that I should say here that I have cracked the not very difficult art of weather forecasting in this most beautiful of countries. I am certain that the weather there is fixed by an Act of Parliament as in summer, one day you will find glorious, warm sunshine to be followed the next day by torrential rain falling endlessly out of leaden skies. The pattern is relentless, and seemingly never changes.

This does mean that on a cycling tour such as I was participating in, you have to wear the correct gear to cycle in, as you could alternate between too warm or being completely underdressed for the deluge that awaits you all too frequently.

The journey from Salzburg to Linz meanders through the Austrian equivalent of the English Lake District; it is gloriously verdant due to the biblical proportions of rain deposited thereon, but the surrounding mountainsides are much higher than anything we have in Britain, and consequently one is treated to magnificent lakeside vistas. The villages alongside these waterfronts are picture-postcard pretty and quite stunning to behold. Throw in a couple of boat journeys across the lakes as part of the onward journey and it becomes idyllic.

When Linz is reached one becomes acquainted with the mighty Danube for the first time. The "Blue Danube" is actually a misnomer as it is uniformly grey, and the phrase owes its creation to its Germanic roots, as the Danube is called the Donau in that language, and the German word for blue is "blau" which of course rhymes with Donau.

The city of Linz is I believe where Hitler was brought up, but I would like to recount the story of how I literally cocked a snook at this malevolent man in my own simplistic little way.

Before I do, I wish to digress slightly by asking you, the reader, if you have taken part in that party game where you are asked to name the three people, from all of history, that you would invite to a dinner party.

My three would be Jesus Christ, because I would love to sit down and just listen to the most famous and charismatic man of all time.

Then it would be Sir Winston Churchill, as I would want to listen to that inspiring rhetoric at first hand.

And finally, my third "guest" would be Adolf Hitler. I would ask him one simple question. "Why?" I have read his book "Mein Kampf" and I have some insight, but in the presence of Jesus Christ I would like to hear him express remorse.

Would I change history if I could? In the case of Hitler most certainly.

Anyway, back my story. I was doing the tourist thing around Vienna and I chanced upon the lodgings that Hitler stayed in during his failed attempt to obtain a place at art college in the city. (No, he wasn't a house painter, he was an artist.)

The address of this room is freely available in all the guidebooks and I found it, late one Saturday afternoon. Everyone had gone home from this "tourist site" but the door to the apartment was still open and I wandered in. I couldn't gain access to the room itself but the door to the loo was ajar, and I wandered in and duly relieved myself in Hitler's toilet, which to me, was highly symbolic. Take that action how you will, but I know what it signified to me!

Tackling the Danube was the next part of this epic journey, and joining the cycle path, having already covered about 120 miles across good old Oesterreich, you set off eastwards for a good few days' ride. Here you follow the route of the great river, stopping off at welcoming towns and villages *en route*, such as the one where the Spargl Restaurant is the best place around.

Spargl is the German word for asparagus, and every course on the menu, be it *hors d'oeuvres*, main course or dessert was asparagus-based. I went through the card, and that day has fuelled my love of the springtime vegetable which is grown in such abundance nearer home in the Vale of Evesham. No eatery was ever more aptly named!

I pulled in a little further down the river's course at the concentration camp at Mauthausen. This place is situated at the top of a steep hill, and straining to get my hybrid bike up there I snapped the gear cable. Which meant that I was confined to a single gear for the rest of the trip; but compared to the account of the suffering I was about to be told about, it was nothing. There, for the Grace of God, go I.

I have been before to one of these camps, the one at Sachsenhausen, a little way north of Berlin, not far from the Polish frontier, and I contend that everyone should, if at all possible, visit one to see the true horror of that black time in our modern history. I experienced at first hand the aura of inhuman suffering and death that still exude from these places One's emotions are laid bare as you witness the tangible evidence of man's total inhumanity to man. I pray to God that no excesses remotely as bad as those which were perpetrated in these camps ever besmirch this planet again.

Being at heart, a pacifist, I would prefer to see disputes settled peaceably across the table but I know that mankind has still not learnt the lessons of centuries of horror. I prayed that day in Mauthausen. What were Hitler and the Nazis thinking?

How could killing on such a gigantic scale have provided us with a better world?

*

Before you, the reader, continue with my writings, please take a minute out now and say a prayer to your own God for the souls that were lost in these places, and that they have found comfort in a better place. And please let nothing remotely like this ever happen to humanity again. Ever.

*

I neared Vienna and the itinerary provided by the tour operator made available train tickets for the last 50 kilometres into Vienna. Why, I asked myself? This is the last phase of an epic ride, a wonderful holiday, and they want to deprive us of our triumphant entry into the old Habsburg capital? Not on your nelly, scoffed I, as I tore up my train ticket. No-one is going to deny me my moment of glory, and I set off for what was the last couple of hours of the holiday.

One enters Vienna on this route by the towpaths of the built-up banks of the Danube, and the old, historic buildings start to take shape in front of your very eyes. Then the final gentle incline as you come up from the river to street level, a ride through the grand streets; and then you are at your hotel, where you say goodbye to your bike which has served you well over the past few days, as you wait for it to be collected by the train-loving tour operators.

Then, it is celebration time, and before dinner (which can only be Wiener Schnitzel followed by Apfel Strudel), you find the world-renowned Café Sacher, where you have one of the most famous confectionaries ever invented, the Sacher Torte, at the very place of its genesis. And boy, have you earned it!

Here comes the usual question, would I do it again? You bet your bottom dollar I would, and how!

The only other country I have cycled in so far is the Caribbean island of Antigua. In the successive years of 2019 and 2020 I have been fortunate enough to spend January out there in the warmth and the sunshine as guests of my other half Liz's son, who is working out there on a long-term contract to improve the roads on behalf of the Antiguan government.

In both visits I was offered the unrestricted use of her son's full carbon BMC road bike, so I was probably astride the best bike on the island whilst riding what are indisputably the worst roads I have ever seen in my life. The pothole seems to be naturally at home here, and the depths that some of them reach are positively, or should I say in this case, negatively, cavernous. And with the tropical rains of January here they are full of water, so that if you cycle into one you haven't a clue whether it is just your tyre which will be submerged, or you will be in it saddle-deep.

One of these potholes was so large and deep that instead of alerting road users with a traffic cone or a flag, which is the logical way of alerting the poor road user, someone put a car seat in it. This, of course, prolonged the useful working life of this specific car seat, which must have feared the worst when it parted company with the car it was attached to; but the whole concept of showing where the pothole is by this method is so ludicrous as to be truly comical.

I for one think it is atypically Antiguan. If Antigua ever has a landslide onto the road, they might well mark the spot with a double decker bus, if the current warning proportions and perspectives are maintained. One of the locals did opine to me that it is a two-edged sword, because if the roads are improved (how could they not be?) then the locals would simply drive faster. Still, I wish them First World road surfaces on which to purvey their Third World driving skills.

On the island of Antigua the daytime temperature here swings violently between 27.9 °and 28.1° Celsigrade (!) Similarly, at night time, it varies between 21.9° and 22.1°. So it is warm all day and every night. Which was wonderful because after all, it was January.

The sun shone relentlessly yet, and here's the rub, there were rain showers every day. Usually a shower would approach stealthily out of nowhere, deposit its load, sometimes violently for two minutes maximum, and then leave the sun to continue its rudely-interrupted work. This explains why Antigua and other Caribbean islands are so verdant.

The constant heat contributes to the pace of life there, which could accurately be described as on the sluggish side of pedestrian. An example of this was when I went to the local bike shop to have an adjustment made to my machine by a mechanic, and I enquired of the lady on the till if such a skilled worker was available. At least 45 seconds elapsed in which time she appeared to become comatose, and I was on the point of searching frantically for the defibrillator, when one of her facial muscles twitched, indicating life, and she gave me the earth-shattering news that a mechanic wasn't available at that time.

I didn't want to ask her when one might next be available, as I couldn't afford the time to hang around for the answer. This lady appears to have several sisters who all seem to have cash desk jobs around the island.

I cycled around Antigua and my wrists ached from bunny-hopping the bike around the thousands of potholes (and the multiplicity of speedbumps) which bedevilled the roads. I concentrated on climbing the hills for my training and the warm weather on my bare legs and arms was absolute bliss.

It is also the custom in Antigua for a car to pip its horn before they overtake you. Which makes some sense, although if adopted in the UK, would cause ructions as cyclists do not take kindly to this sort of treatment from British motorists. The Highway Code is still waiting to be published in Antigua.

Other obstacles are the herds of sheep, goats and cows who wander around freely on the grass verges at roadside, and the number of dogs who go berserk and yap frighteningly at you as you cycle past them is nobody's business.

One of the cutest features of cycling around Antigua is that from time to time on the coastal roads the streetlamps change to a deep red lustre, which is totally different to the normal yellow, orange or even icy blue bulbs one might encounter elsewhere.

These red lights are to avoid confusing the local sea turtle population into thinking that it is still daytime, and thus dissuading them from attempting to cross the busy roads at night in order to reach the saltwater lagoons on the other side of the road. These creatures sensibly sleep during the night so do not want to become befuddled into thinking it is still daylight by the bright streetlamps.

There are also road signs indicating "Sea Turtle Crossing" but I think these are a waste of money, as I am not aware that any sea turtles can read!

During the two Januarys I spent in Antigua I clocked up a thousand miles on the bike, which included conquering the feared Fig Tree Drive in both directions, so I was a happy cyclist.

It is a small world, but as I go deeper into my dotage it would be lovely to think that I can see more of it and above all, cycle in different countries and continents. I hope God spares me long enough to accomplish this.

CHAPTER ELEVEN

I Become a Teacher of Cycling

When my days in the world of banking (yawn, yawn!) and financial advising (dangerous territory!) came to an end as I breasted the retirement age tape, I still felt that I wanted to keep active. Therefore it was somewhat fortuitous that an advertisement for a course to train cycling instructors caught my eye, so I looked at it in more detail as this sounded like a wonderful way to occupy oneself gainfully.

It transpired that the advert was placed by Wolverhampton City Council, and they were running a four-day course to train Instructors for the Bikeability scheme, which is all about teaching schoolchildren the rudiments of cycling. Ah, I surmised, it's the old Cycling Proficiency Scheme under a sexier title. Well, yes and no.

I remember as a 12-year-old myself being put through my paces on the school playground and passing the Cycling Proficiency Test, and getting one of those wonderful circular metal badges for the handlebars of my bike together with a certificate. I still have the certificate, what a portent of things to come that was! Happy days – except that as I recall the instructors left you with the instruction to get out onto the road and put your newly found knowledge of the Highway Code into action.

The problem with that, for me, was that I saw it as a major stumbling block, the fact that we had been nowhere near the road and those big moving things they call, now what did they say it was? Ah yes, traffic!!! Alarm bells ringing for every child in those far off days and for decades to follow, because having been cosseted somewhat on the playground, none of us had even tried riding on the road.

But back to the advert. Bikeability had rebranded itself after what must have been some careful thinking by its organisers, and was now delivering its training of the present-day generation of cyclists actually on the road, which made a whole heap of sense to me, for one.

The whole concept sounded very interesting, so I signed up for the course, which was to be run in November 2013, some six years after I had first become a serious rider. I learnt an awful lot of the most useable information as well from this course. 50 per cent was theory, such as how to and how not to deliver the teaching points, and 50 per cent was practical, by getting out onto the roads and delivering a mock lesson.

Bikeability provides awards to its trainees at three levels. Level One is delivered wholly on the playground. This is where the trainees demonstrate that they can actually handle their bikes, by making them go where they want them to go, and that they can efficiently use their brakes and gears, as well as being able to look behind while still in control of their bikes whilst moving forward and signalling, simultaneously riding one handed. In other words, the basics of riding a bike. The Level One part of the Bikeability syllabus equates to all intents and purposes to the now defunct Cycling Proficiency Scheme.

Those who impress sufficiently on the playground therefore tackle Level Two, which sees our would-be cyclists venture out onto the road. Here they are the given the skills to cope with traffic, turning left and right into and out of main and side roads, executing U-turns, and signalling to traffic and other road users at the appropriate times.

Level Three is what I would broadly term town centre riding, where we encounter traffic lights, roundabouts, multi-lane systems and we learn how to use cycle lanes, bus lanes and advanced cycle boxes and the yellow hashed boxes at traffic lights.

Back to my instructor course in Wolverhampton. The day of the Level Three practical dawned, if you could call it that, and provided us with weather on which it wasn't safe to open the front door, let alone climb on a bike. It fairly lashed it down all day, but that didn't stop about 20 of us, that is our teaching instructors and us their pupils, from parading around the city centre of Wolverhampton in one long hi-viz-clad snake, which is the official Bikeability jargon for a controlled line of riders.

Despite the torrent of rain which was drenching us we managed to complete our training. Little did I know then that this type of weather was never going to be a reason to prevent us from taking schoolchildren out on the highways and by-ways of this blessed country of ours. Oh no, the show must go on, folks. Always.

I duly passed the course and was made a National Standards Instructor Provisional (NSIP) with the proviso that I would be observed in action within six months of my pressing the "go" button. Then, if all was well, I would drop the P for Provisional and shed my learner plates (that is an awful mixed metaphor, I know) and become an A for Actual, thus an NSIA.

Because I wasn't ready to start work immediately as a Bikeability Instructor due to my finishing off as an independent financial advisor, I then began in earnest the following September (2014). Not with Wolverhampton City Council, but with Birmingham City Council, which would provide me with work much nearer home.

My very first week as a Bikeability instructor was undertaken as an assistant to the guy who organised the rota for Birmingham City Council Bikeability instructors, and it was a very informative assignment for me.

This particular instructor had completed the Land's End to John O'Groats ride (known to cyclists as LEJOG) during the August holidays, and this ride is on my bucket list of things to do on a bike (see earlier in the book!).

I enquired of him how much weight he shed during this adventure, and he told me that he actually gained weight by virtue of the amount of calories he was shoe-horning down his gullet at the end of each day's riding. Note to self – don't use LEJOG to become sylph-like!

Anyway, after that week I was up and running and being employed as a "professional" cyclist, that is to say, I was being paid for doing something I love. Yes, I know, it is a bit of an exaggeration, but in some small way it is true!

Week upon week followed and I was now part of the rota as regular assignments as an Assistant Instructor filled my diary. I passed (seamlessly, he says) from an NSIP to an NSIA which meant that I was now available to be a Lead Instructor, thus allowing me to be the guy running the show at a Bikeability booking in a school. I like to think that I took this in my stride, as my love of the bike and now the ability to pass on this passion to youngsters, was showing through in my work.

It is very interesting the way one develops a script for delivering this teaching, and I was gleaning the best bits of what I was seeing and hearing from the different instructors I was assigned to. One of my favourite instructors to work with was a guy named Alan Baxter, who hailed from the Grimsby area. He was exactly a year younger than me, which made us the two oldest instructors on the Birmingham strength. He had a way of verbally getting across his points at every given Bikeability learning point, and the jigsaw of my developing presentation script owed more and more to his delivery than that of anyone else.

I was, and may I say it, for the first time in my working life, gaining some respect from my peers. I am sure this was due to the fact that I was, at last, in my dotage, doing something that I enjoyed, instead of the mountains of paperwork which dogged my deskbound careers in both the bank and as an independent financial adviser.

So much so, that when I broke my wrist in that little old crash during a time trial in 2017, to keep me gainfully occupied I was invited into the Council Office to run the Bikeability "show". This was a generous offer from the Council, and one for which I was grateful I undertook to work through the months of July and August whilst my wrist mended to the condition where I could climb back onto my bike and resume my outdoor work as an Instructor.

Working for and alongside the Project Manager gave me a huge insight into how the Council, who were the providers of the Bikeability Scheme to the schools, interacted with the Department for Transport, the Governmental body who allocate the life-giving funds to make the whole thing tick. I even acquired a new skill, which was that of writing with my right hand (me being left-handed), as my broken left wrist was in plaster for a minimum of six weeks. An ambidexter at my time of life!

Shortly after I was fit enough to resume instructing, the time came for me to move down south to Surrey and I found, to my great fortune, or so I thought, an advert from Surrey County Council asking for an experienced Bikeability Instructor. Bingo! "I am in here", I thought, and I duly fired off my CV via an email to the relevant person. Now I was confident my CV would see me walk into this post, as I was a Lead Instructor with three years' full time experience, I had actually worked for those two months as a Scheme Administrator for Birmingham, and I was a racing cyclist who averaged 1,000 miles a month without the slightest drama.

Imagine my utter consternation when the emailed reply from Surrey rejected me with the added 'insult' that I didn't meet their criteria! What! Who the hell were they hoping to employ, Bradley Wiggins? Or maybe they had Brad on their strength and then, yes, my criteria wouldn't stand up to his, as the last time I looked I couldn't find any Olympic Gold Medals on my sideboard.

Was I downhearted? You bet your bottom dollar I was, and with my confidence dented, I looked at the map to see what counties shared a boundary with Surrey. I found the address for West Sussex County Council (WSCC) and fired off my now rejected CV, and to my eternal thanks they replied by return, and asked when I could come and talk to them! Which I did, and I am with WSCC at the time of writing and loving every minute of it. I have even moved from being an NSIA to an NSIT, which means that I have qualified to train new Instructors.

One other part of the Bikeability job is to deliver training on Balance Bikes, that is small bikes without pedals, to the four and five-year olds in the school reception classes around West Sussex. These tiny machines have replaced stabilisers in the process of learning to ride and serve a great purpose, as in my humble opinion, stabilisers provide a false of security to tiny tots learning to ride.

I have seen one four-year-old girl refuse to the point of screaming the place down when it was suggested that she had the stabilisers removed from her bike after I had noticed that neither of them was actually touching the floor, due to their being fitted incorrectly. After some diversionary tactics the offending "aids" were removed and without drawing her attention to their removal, off she rode happily into the sunset having been able to balance and ride all along without realising it. Ditch the stabilisers, and crack on with actually getting these little ones to ride properly has to be the best way forward.

One also delivers Learn to Ride sessions to young children, usually from the ages of 6 to 10 or 11, and occasionally to adults. I have not found anything as emotionally gratifying as the moment when a youngster finally shakes of all their doubts and worries and rides a bike properly.

For me that moment is without parallel in teaching Bikeability, and whenever I am successful in passing on this wonderful gift of balance to a new cyclist, I still feel an amazing tingle.

The first time I taught a youngster to ride I sat in my car and had trouble holding back tears of joy. And the look on their grateful parents' faces says it all.

These Balance Bike sessions are actually the greatest of fun, as the happy-go-lucky four-year-olds present themselves to you on the playground and we engage in games such as Grandma's Footsteps, What's the time, Mr Wolf?, Rocket Ships, and Excuse Me. Take my word for it, the participation by these tiny tots in these games on their balance bikes is nothing short of hilarious. The expressions on their little faces tell it all; they love their bikes and they are joining a privileged band of people who can ride a bike.

Before one can start work as a Bikeability Instructor then your prospective employer has to do a DBS (Disclosure and Barring Service) check on you to ensure that there are no incidents against your name which would render you unsuitable to undertake the considerable responsibility and trust of being in charge of children. Like teachers, we are alone with minors when delivering these sessions and act *in loco parentis*. This DBS clean bill of health is something which we all jealously look after.

One is always open to abuse from one's fellow road users, i.e. car drivers who obviously know better than we, the Instructors. I was once teaching on the main road part of a T-junction opposite the side road turn outside a school in Birmingham when a car came screaming along the road towards me and my trainees before coming to a less than graceful, screeching, shuddering halt at the mouth of the T-junction.

"Allo", thought I, "Do we have a problem here?", as the driver's window whirred down and an Afro hairstyle, rapidly followed by its owner, stuck its head out? "Why you teaching these kids here man, it's dangerous, get back on de playground!" he intoned. Quick as a flash, I retorted "And where did you learn to drive your car with such due care and attention? On a supermarket car park after it closed, or actually on the road?"

He flashed me with a look that said "You'll keep", and away he went on his merry way with a screech of the tyres that left a smoky imprint in the tarmac. Some people are absolutely clueless.

I have a similar rejoinder to car drivers who race up to me on my bike at red traffic lights and try to take up my space. I have a habit of tapping on their windows, and when I have grabbed their oh so valuable attention, I ask "Show me the title deeds, then". Which brings the response "What the (insert your own expletive here!) are you talking about?" "Well you obviously own the road!" is my follow-up. Smart Alec doesn't do it justice! It's not exactly "Live at the Apollo" standard, but it makes me feel better, and that I have got a very important point across to these brainless idiots who quite simply resent sharing their (!) roads with cyclists.

Just recently I was delivering a 1-2-1 lesson at Level 2 to a 12-year-old African boy who possessed a very shy and retiring personality. We had stopped in a side street whilst I was outlining a teaching point to him, when a lad of about 11 or 12 years old rode by us on his bike and yelled at me "Have I passed?"

Seeing the humour of the situation I smiled in his direction, acknowledging his harmless comment. But a couple of minutes later he cycled past us again in the opposite direction, this time executing a wheelie, and again enquiring whether or not he had passed. As I didn't want this lad to become a distraction I simply said "No, leave us to it now and move on". Whereupon he stopped and rode back up to me, accompanied by several of his contemporaries who had appeared, it seemed, out of nowhere. Later I speculated that they had crawled out from under the stones where they live (portent of things to come?).

"Who are you telling to move on, it's a free country!" he said to me face to face. I thought to myself "Here we go."

I have never enjoyed or subscribed to the free country argument or understood what is meant by it so I started to reason with him, telling him that I was teaching a trainee and we didn't need any distractions, thank you very much for asking.

"We live in this road and you can't tell us what to do." He continued with notable verbal skill and dexterity as he warmed to his subject. To my amazement he was now standing nose to nose with me and started to push me in the chest. Eleven years old and full of it! The language of these morons (Objection - sorry that sounds biased. Objection sustained as that is unfair to morons) then deteriorated to gutter level and they had obviously just discovered the 'F' word as they were using it adjectivally, as a verb and a noun and also as every alternate word in the garbage that was now spilling forth from their twisted minds.

The 'F' word was also one of the more socially acceptable words they were using. "How proud your parents must be of all of you," I mused *a propos* of nothing to myself.

This situation was now deteriorating rapidly and I was anxious that it didn't develop into a racially-motivated incident against the African lad I was instructing so I kept him away from the epicentre. One of the neanderthals (Objection – that still sounds biased. Objection sustained as that is unfair to neanderthals) then started to fire a retractable catapult at my chest. This contraption had a sort of ball on the end of its elastic and when it hit its target, my chest, would rebound back to its owner who would repeat the process, thereby making him look macho to his idiotic accomplices.

Meanwhile, behind me, someone was whacking me on the helmet repeatedly with another object. Whilst neither of these activities hurt as such, they would not have been my chosen method of relaxation that afternoon. So there I was, being verbally abused by one knuckle-dragger (yes, I know!), hit in the chest by matey with his catapult thingy and bashed on the bonce from behind by Little Lord Fauntleroy, or whatever he called himself.

I had a choice, and it wasn't an easy one. I could use physical force to repel these downright nasty characters or stand there and take it (metaphorically) on the chin until the whole situation blew itself out. I had to take the latter option, because if I had had recourse to the former then I would have been dismissed from my job with a DBS record up in smoke, and probably a criminal assault charge on minors to answer.

It was, of course an easy choice to make because I value and love my job, but it was extremely unpleasant while it lasted, as the last straw was when Matey Boy, he who instigated the whole thing, put his hand into the inside pocket of his jacket, making as if he couldn't quite pull out the knife with which he said he was going to cut me.

"You having problems there?" I enquired helpfully, as I let my guard slip for the one and only time. He then issued me with an invitation to follow him to his house where he would run the bread knife through me. I declined his kind offer, and felt it was about time this whole sorry pantomime was ended. Brushing through them, and there were about eight of them, I collected my trainee and we moved a few streets away to another location, where we finished the lesson in rather surreal circumstances.

I had another 1-2-1 lesson to move onto after this awful episode and when I got back to my car, I had to take a moment as what had happened suddenly washed over me. I sat there shaking like a leaf for five or 10 minutes before I was able to collect myself and get back into my day's work. I reported the incident in full to my employers who were most supportive and for which I was grateful.

This whole deplorable happening did not shake my resolve with regard to delivering Bikeability, but it is something I have no wish to experience again. I know one or two instructors, no names, no pack drill, (again I haven't a clue what that means, either), who would have walked away from that incident, brushing their hands together and stepping over a pile of corpses on the way to their next

1-2-1. I am joking, of course. They might have retaliated by using the pack drill (!) on them!

There is a book in itself in Bikeability and one day soon I may write it, but for now, I will keep on delivering the scheme and savouring every moment.

CHAPTER TWELVE

Thrills and Spills on and off the Bike

Unfortunately, it is not possible to cycle the volume of miles that I have nor the number of races I have completed without undergoing several crashes, slips and falls.

My first such mishap was the one in the student zone in Cardiff which I have chronicled elsewhere. My next encounter with the tarmac could be attributed entirely to the evils of black ice. I had a circuit in Cardiff which I would train on in the early daylight hours, and one freezing morning I chose to turn off the main roads, which had been salted or gritted and were perfectly safe to ride on, and turned left into a side street to take a shortcut home. The road surface was black and frost free, or so I thought; and as I turned the handlebars the bike shot from underneath me on the tarmac, which was slick with lethal black ice. My body slid across the road as I parted company painfully with the bike. Memo to self, beware of black ice.

On the same circuit I again parted company with my steed when, on a sunny Sunday morning, and again turning left, the front wheel skidded across a patch of loose grit and I came down with a horrible bump, suffering road rash on my hip through torn Lycra. I didn't realise that I had lost my house keys during this incident, finding this out only when I returned home. I hurriedly retraced my steps and luckily the bunch of keys was still lying in the road where they had come to rest some half an hour previously. Memo to self, beware of patches of loose grit.

Coming off the bike at any time can be an experience fraught with pain, and it is certainly to be avoided whenever possible.

Such as when I was back in Birmingham and on another of my training circuits. This one was a rectangle with four tight 90° left hand turns which I would take at the fastest speed I could muster. On one of these turns I shot around the corner at some velocity, only to find myself hurtling towards a car approaching the same junction. Both and the driver and I slammed our anchors, on but my back wheel skidded alarmingly, and dumped me on the floor, sliding on my side towards the wheels of the car. I came to rest within a yard of his front wheels. I picked myself up, thoroughly embarrassed by what had been too fast a cornering manoeuvre by me, thus causing this nasty incident. Again, road rash but this tumble could have been much, much worse. Memo to self, be bloody careful!

On holiday in North Devon, I was making an exploratory circuit of Ilfracombe, which is one of the steepest holiday resorts in the whole of the UK. This is all the more mysterious, since it is full of retired people, whose climbing skills, on foot obviously, are tested to the full by the incredible hills between the promenade and the town centre.

I thought I would test my own climbing prowess (which at the time hadn't manifested itself,) and turned left up a street that looked steep, which turned out to be a massive understatement to say the least. I remained seated in the saddle initially, then I had to stand up; and then the front wheel started proving difficult to keep on the ground so that I was now in danger of tipping over backwards.

As I was cleated in it, was going to prove too difficult to get my feet out of the pedals in time to prevent myself from ending up on the floor, so I made a decision that I had to throw myself onto the grass verge at the side of the road to give myself a soft landing. I succeeded with this method of dismounting and I walked away unhurt but chastened, in that there were still gradients that I just couldn't conquer.

But in one of my time trials in 2017 I was involved in a mother and father of a crash, and I suffered an awful injury which whilst not life-threatening, kept me out of racing for 11 months. I was taking part in the usual Tuesday night time trial on the A435 in Worcestershire, a race organised for six months of the year on Tuesday evenings by my club the Warwickshire Road Club, and one in which I had ridden dozens of times.

The course itself involved tearing up and down the A435 twice in each direction, with a left turn at approximately halfway into a banjo-shaped spur to ensure that we completed the full 10 miles. This left turn had a petrol station set at 45°across the turn which necessitated the competitors being extra vigilant as they hurtled around the corner at top speed.

Any cars coming out of the petrol station would have to look to their right to see whether there were any cyclists bearing down on them. This situation had produced many hairy moments during these races, and many was the story that would be recounted after the event back at the Warwickshire Road Club's clubroom of that particular evening's close shaves with disaster at this location.

And then one balmy Tuesday night the inevitable happened. And inevitably, it happened to me. It was June 20st, the day before the longest day of the year and coincidentally it also was the warmest, with the temperature at 8 p.m. still way in excess of 30°. There was a public house directly opposite the petrol station, and it was packed out with thirsty customers who were all out on the pavement watching the racing on this exceptional evening.

I was actually on for a season's best on the course, as I had just mentally checked my progress as I sped through the four-mile mark, and I moved into the slip road to the left of the dual carriageway ready to swing through the 90° turn. As I negotiated the curve I glanced up and saw, to my horror, a car pulling out of the petrol station forecourt and positioned broadside across the road blocking my path.

Everything from then on seemed to happen in slow motion although in reality it could only have been a split second. I had a decision to make, and fast! There wasn't enough time to apply my brakes, as I would probably skid and lose control of the bike. Therefore should I swerve to my left and go behind the car, probably mounting the pavement whilst doing so and risking an out of control wobble, or should I swerve to my right and try and go round the front of the car, which would, of course still itself be moving to my right?

Or so I thought. The car was actually stationary as I believe the lady driver saw me and froze. In the aforementioned split second I did slam my brakes, on but as she was going nowhere I hit her front wheel arch at a speed well in excess of 25 miles per hour.

I shot over the handlebars, somersaulted and landed on the bonnet of her car, then my momentum and speed sent me hurtling into another somersault, and I came to rest in the sitting position, but with the force of the impact jack-knifing my body weight totally onto my left arm, which crashed into the kerbstone. As I came to rest at the feet of the horrified pub drinkers, the rest of me slammed down with my left wrist underneath me, the weight of my body breaking my left wrist and dislocated it horribly.

My bike, with its tyres pumped up to about 130 pounds per square inch rebounded backwards off the tyre of the car, landing many yards away from where I was now lying in a crumpled heap.

My first thought was that my season was probably over. Not that I would know for certain, but I can believe that people have the daftest, most irrelevant thoughts at moments like this. I had remained conscious during the whole impact, and then I looked down at my left wrist, which I guessed was broken but was also pointing in the wrong direction; and I hadn't a clue as to what that meant.

The drinkers were now mobilising themselves and one or two people were cradling me and asking if I was comfortable.

I was spread-eagled across the gutter and the pavement but I don't think I have ever been more comfortable, thank you very much for asking. There were women who were nurses, men who were doctors and loads of people who were volunteering to be witnesses and of immediate help to me, but I was satisfied with just lying there.

Eventually after 45 minutes the ambulance arrived and I was carefully placed in it for onward transport to the hospital. I pleaded with the driver not to go over any bumps in the road and also gave them the news that if I couldn't see where I was going, and I couldn't, then I was likely to be travel sick!

X-rays and painkillers were administered as I lay on a bed in the A & E section of the hospital, having had my beautiful Warwickshire Road Club all in one skinsuit cut off me. Confirmation arrived that I had indeed broken my left wrist, as well as the little finger on my right hand. Then there was the problem of the dislocation as my left wrist was still hanging off at right angles.

In time a doctor came in to my own private little torture chamber, and said with a smile on his face "Ah yes, we have a dislocation to relocate before we can go any further". At which point the nurse, who was a lady of robust cheerfulness, said to me that would be probably be more painful than anything I had ever experienced. Which I thought, for a lady of her knowhow, was a fairly strange way of putting me at my ease!

Anyway, I believed her, and was mightily relieved when she injected me full of painkillers. The doctor explained to me how he was going to accomplish the relocation of my wrist, and I thought he said he was going to push my shoulder away from my wrist with one of his hands while he pulled my wrist in the opposite direction. To my consternation I had, in fact, heard him correctly.

He began to push my shoulder backwards and then pulled my broken wrist towards him in the opposite direction. The painkillers were doing their job as I hadn't yet shot off the bed and hit the ceiling when suddenly, there was a click, akin to a Lego brick slotting into place. "There she goes," he said in his "all in a day's work" voice, and wished me good luck with my rehabilitation as he swept out of the room.

Honestly, I never felt a thing. At least all my limbs were now pointing in the correct direction and all that was needed was for my arm to be put in plaster. 12 hours after being admitted to hospital, I was on my way home.

I knew I needed legal representation, because I was going to have to sue the driver of the car for damages and the loss of earnings during my enforced absence from work. I was a member of British Cycling (BC), who offered and advertised the use of a solicitor in the event of a cycling accident, so I duly contacted them.

The law firm of BC's recommendation listened patiently as I recounted the events of my accident. Then blow me down, they said they wouldn't represent me as they considered I didn't have more than a 50% chance of winning the lawsuit! Utterly bemused by this statement, I toyed with the idea of sending British Cycling an email of complaint after what I considered was reprehensible treatment and a waste of my subscription. I didn't, because it all seemed like too much trouble and I needed to find a lawyer quickly to get the ball rolling.

I searched through the comic, the affectionate name which cyclists bestow upon "Cycling Weekly", and found a firm of solicitors who said they specialised in cycling accidents. Furthermore, in a telephone conversation they told me that all of their firm's partners were, indeed, racing cyclists themselves. This boosted my flagging spirits and they took on my case. After what seemed like an eternity, but was in fact, 15 months they won my case for me and I was awarded in excess of £11,000 pounds. That softened the blow!

The accident has left me with a permanently weakened left wrist, but to date it has not prevented me from resuming my time trialling career, even if I find taking the lid off a honey jar extremely difficult, which ultimately might be good for my weight!

CHAPTER TWELVE and a BIT*

Proud to be Purple

I have mentioned before my one sibling, my older brother Roger, who was born in 1945 some five and a half years before I (dis)graced the world in November 1950. Roger was a competent footballer and cricketer and a very competitive cross-country runner, representing the county at the latter discipline.

We both attended Holly Lodge County Grammar School for Boys in Smethwick, and on one auspicious occasion Roger was well out in front during the school cross-country championship race. The underlying prize in this race was to determine which of the four houses; our house Warwick, or one of the other three, Stratford, Kenilworth or Ludlow, would win the school cross country shield by virtue of scoring the fewest points. Points being allocated as one point for the first runner home, two for the second, three for the third and so on, with the house which had amassed the fewest points holding the shield aloft.

So as Roger approached the school drive in a clear lead he was ordered by his house Master, Mr Burgess, to slow down and allow the second runner, Kenny Tedstone, or Kenneth Andrew Marjorebanks Tedstone to give him his full monicker, to catch him so that they could cross the line together in a dead heat and nail down only one point each, totalling two, instead of three points for first and second positions. Cunning plot eh?

Roger somewhat reluctantly and frustratingly obeyed team orders, and he and Kenny duly contrived the dead heat.

*Author's Note – This Chapter is numbered in line with my obsessive superstitious nature (before you ask!)

Whereupon Roger was informed that he (and Kenny) had equalled (not beaten) the school cross country course record. He was, however, completely hacked off because he had been told to slow down, and could have smashed the record on his own had he not allowed the following Kenny to cross the line with him. It was no surprise therefore to find that Roger forsook footie, cricket and cross-country running to take up that prince of sports, cycling.

At the age of 14 the County Borough of Smethwick Education Conmmittee allowed you to undergo a medical in order to be given clearance to take on a newspaper delivery round, which was usually one's first remunerated job, Passing the medical, as I mentioned in Chapter One, Roger duly presented himself for paper round duties at Riddell's Newsagents near the top (or southern) end of the Bearwood Road, just before its crossroads at the landmark of the King's Head public house, on the Hagley Road.

One of his colleagues as a paperboy was his great mate Roy Dursley, known to all and sundry as Bong, and they had been through primary school, grammar school and the church choir at St Mary's Church in Bearwood together. Not only did they both work for Riddell's, but they rode together to and from school, which was a daily return trip comprising five further undulating miles.

All of this rendered them both supremely fit. As they couldn't get no (sic) satisfaction from the aforementioned sports, their attention turned to the sport of cycling, and in particular, the proximity of the outdoor banked velodrome less than five miles away at the Halesowen Cycling Club, which became an irresistible temptation.

This famous club was fortunate in that it was, and to this day, remains, I believe, the only cycling club in the whole of the United Kingdom which owns its own velodrome. Other such cycling arenas, such as there are, are owned usually by local councils who rent the premises and facilities to the cycling clubs.

Halesowen is a town historically in north Worcestershire, not that far from the centre of Birmingham, so its catchment area has always been a large one, taking in the whole of the west and south of Birmingham and the towns comprising the industrial area known as the Black Country. Any cyclist, therefore, who had pretentions to ride on this banked track therefore joined Halesowen Cycling Club, making its membership an elite who's who of competitive cyclists in the area.

The club have always ridden in bright purple cycling attire and have adopted the motto "Proud to be Purple". One current member who is Proud to be Purple is William Fotheringham, the UK's foremost author on the sport of cycling, no mean track cyclist himself among the veteran ranks, albeit a few age categories below me! The club's Patron is the legendary cycling World Champion Hugh Porter, who hails from Wolverhampton, and is himself married to Olympic Gold Medal swimmer Anita Lonsborough.

Returning to the times of the late fifties and early sixties Roger, Bong and two other mates, Martyn Rouse and Keith Graham, joined the club, having invested some of their hard-earned paper round cash in track bikes.

Track bikes have no brakes and have a fixed wheel, which means one can't freewheel or pedal backwards. At the age of 15 Roger was now training with some of the best riders in the country, and the sprint became his forte.

The sprint event comprises a race of three laps of the 400 metre velodrome, with the first rider past the post taking home the spoils. But that is not the true story of the sprint, because the first two laps are generally conducted at snail's pace, as no-one wants to be the one who burns his boats by breaking for home, and running out of energy as the finishing line approaches.

In those days riders were allowed to do a "track stand", which basically meant standing up on the pedals and balancing, going absolutely bloody nowhere, until your opponent weakened and was forced to make the first move. This led to unlikely but true scenarios where track stands were executed for anything up to 45 minutes, yes minutes! This did nothing to make the erroneously named sprints a great spectacle for the paying public, but it is only in the last decade that such track stands have been limited to 30 seconds, yes seconds, before the race commissaire declares the race null and void and orders a rerun.

The big hitter, the top man at Halesowen Cycling Club in those days was a wiry sprinter named Roy Hurdley, who was one of the leading sprinters in the land at the time. He was good enough to represent England in the 1962 Commonwealth Games in Kingston, Jamaica, so Halesowen CC looked up to Roy Hurdley with justifiable awe.

Roger was training more and more with the elite group of the sprinters, and this was sharpening him nicely in readiness for sprinting races ahead. In 1961 Roger's stated aim was the National Schoolboy Sprint Championship, for which he was training himself to win. Come the day of the big event and…

… he missed it through illness. A lad named Pete Jenner from Portsmouth won the Championship and Roger was thwarted.

Then one fateful weekend Pete Jenner showed up at the Salford Bridge track (now defunct) in Birmingham. Mom, Dad and I attended this meeting in support of our Roger, and we were positioned above the final bend looking directly down the final straight.

Six riders set off for that sprint race, and the first lap as expected took a month of Sundays to complete, during which every rider kept a strict watching brief on all of their rivals. The second lap was nearing its completion as the final bend loomed for the penultimate time when, right in front of my disbelieving eyes, one rider made the jump and the others responded instantly.

Suddenly, with a sickening sound of groaning riders and tangling metal four, of the sprinters collided and came down together and pandemonium broke loose. Such was the force of the crash that there was blood and gore and broken bikes everywhere, and one bike frame actually snapped in half.

But two riders escaped the melee, Roger and one other, and they set off on the one final lap which would see them home. Skilfully avoiding the carnage which had happened on that final bend less than 30 seconds before, Roger held off his rival and was declared the winner, thus defeating National Schoolboy Champ Pete Jenner into the bargain. This race wasn't committed to posterity by being filmed, but if you watch the 1967 Grand National on You Tube this was when all the horses except one, Foinavon, failed to negotiate one of the closing fences. Eventually only one more horse, Honey End, scrambled over this fence at the second attempt and set off in forlorn and ultimately unsuccessful pursuit of Foinavon, who won the world's most famous steeplechase at odds of 100-1.

The final stages of any fiercely-contested sprint race can be alarming as elbows, knees and even heads can be deployed to put your opponent off, and this race had shown what a dangerous activity this could be. To add grist to Roger's mill he met Pete Jenner and beat him again that season, thus giving him a two and O win ratio over him. He has always dined out on this proud assertion that he himself, and not Jenner would have been National Schoolboy Champ that year were it not for his illness.

The family used to follow Roger around from track to track supporting him, and I found it all fascinating. Roger used to bring home Cycling Weekly, known to all cycling enthusiasts as "the Comic", from the paper shop, and I used to devour the contents of this magazine as avidly as he did. So I was familiar with the exploits of track stars like Karl Barton, Lloyd Binch and Roy Hurdley himself.

In its pages road racing would be covered, and the Tour de France would be reported in full, chronicling the exploits of top riders such as the ill-fated Tommy Simpson, the trail-blazing Brian Robinson or the legendary Beryl Burton. The great novelty for me was that I could see the track giants who I was reading about in the comic in the flesh at the same meetings where Roger was competing.

When I was about 10 years old in 1961, and loitering without intent at the track watching my older brother train assiduously, it was suggested during a break from their strenuous efforts that I should be placed on a track bike, to put me through my paces and see whether there was any latent talent in my juvenile bones (I don't think I had any cycling muscles at that juncture!).

Logistically, my legs didn't actually reach the pedals as the saddle was set for the big boys, so with a few minor adjustments, and with Roy Hurdley keeping the bike upright by holding the saddle stem, I set off turning the pedals of this fixed wheel track bike. Because Roy was holding me and controlling my (lack of) speed then I travelled at the speed of darkness, which I assume to be the opposite of the speed of light, and then was lifted back off the wheels on to terra firma, probably much to the amusement of those watching.

Did this little episode whet my appetite to get involved in the wonderful world of track cycling? You would think so, wouldn't you? Not a bit of it. I returned to my own little world which had no room for anything other than football or cricket. Little did I know that I would be joining the purple-clad warriors of Halesowen Cycling Club some 49 years later in my own right.

Ultimately the time came when my competitive urges did finally turn to track cycling. For those of you who have never ventured onto a velodrome, please let me outline the differences between an indoor and an outdoor track. The classic distances vary – an outdoor track is of 400 metres distance, with a surface of tarmac, and the rider is also subject to the whims of the wind direction.

This latter fact can have a significant effect on races, as the long straights can deliver either a telling tailwind or a potentially race-changing headwind to help or hinder the rider's progress. No riding takes place when the track is wet, as the plethora of painted lines on the track surface are lethally slippery in the rain. Also, I believe the rider's insurance is negated if they succumb to an accident on a wet track when riding should prudently have been suspended, even temporarily, while the sun dries everything up.

Another difference is that the bankings are shallower outdoors and the straights are certainly longer, and it is on these stretches where race-defining moves are more likely outdoors than indoors.

Whereas indoors the distance of one lap is 250 metres and the banking is much steeper, sometimes over 40°, although there is a track at Southampton where a lap is only 150 metres, and this makes for the most frantic of racing spectacles.

Indoors the surface is comprised of timbered boards, and the relative shortness of the track brings the banking of the bends into play more significantly, as riders bomb down from the top of the banking to make their race-defining efforts.

Due to the effects of centrifugal force, a rider will have to maintain a minimum speed of 22 miles per hour at the top of the bankings to prevent them from sliding down to the well of the track. This slide is not recommended, as it can involve being mown down by following bikes and / or riders, and copious amounts of your own flesh being exposed through torn lycra onto the unforgiving wooden boards.

There is of course no wind assistance indoors (unless someone accidentally or deliberately leaves a door open!), but the air temperature does play its part, as the warmer it is inside the velodrome then the greater the potential for faster times. Controversially, in international events the temperature can be artificially manipulated to give home riders an unfair advantage, and this has been perpetrated on many an occasion during competition (see earlier comment about doors).

While I was living in Cardiff and improving gradually on the local time trialling scene, I was handily placed to use the excellent facilities of the National Velodrome of Wales in Newport, some 12 miles away. My brother, who although he was now some 64 years young, had never really climbed off the bike since his teenage heyday, and he was keen to reignite his own competitive urges by competing once again on the track.

Newport Velodrome is an indoor boarded track with 42° banking. To compete on any indoor track in the United Kingdom a rider has to acquire track accreditation, which is basically a licence to race.

So Roger came down to Newport from his home in Worcestershire every Sunday night for eight weeks to accompany me on the accreditation sessions. These taught one amongst other things how to ride safely in bunches of riders on the track, and how to ascend and descend from the banking and use them to full advantage when picking up speed whilst attacking.

The accreditation course was delivered by Courtney Rowe, a distinguished Welsh rider and cycling coach himself, and father of Luke Rowe, the current road captain of Team INEOS (formerly Team Sky in a previous incarnation). Luke can be seen stage managing the day's racing tactics from within the peloton during races such as the Tour de France.

Courtney was a brilliant trainer and tutor. What he didn't know about the not inconsiderable art of track cycling wasn't worth knowing, and he shared this knowledge with us as he put us through our paces.

There would be anything up to 24 riders undergoing the accreditation process at any one session, and a much-needed discipline was learning how to ride not only tactically in a bunch, but also safely.

When you are careering around the boards at speed, all 24 of you, on fixed wheel bikes with no brakes, you are in such close proximity to one another that if anyone makes an error of judgment by twitching unexpectedly, then everyone can come down, and it then becomes a case of how quickly everyone can be loaded into ambulances.

Our peloton always contained one or two headstrong individuals (nutjobs), who shouldn't really have been let out in public on their own, let alone given control of a dangerous track bike in a fast moving bunch. If Courtney spotted any misdemeanour, however slight, because that was all it took to cause absolute mayhem, then the miscreant was hooked off the track immediately. They would then be stood on the track infield alongside our tutor while they contemplated the error of their ways, and to watch the rest of the bunch showing them how it should be done sensibly. In my view a superb way of teaching the correct track etiquette without anyone finishing up on hospital food. I loved this accreditation course, and so did my big brother.

Learning how to use the banking was an essential part of the course, and Courtney would encourage us with each circuit to gradually mount the inclines until we were riding around the very top. As I have already said one has to maintain a minimum speed of 22 miles per hour to stay on top of the banking otherwise centrifugal force will simply force you to slide down to the bottom of the track, leaving quantities of lycra and your own skin on the boards, never a pleasant experience.

But once you were on top of the banking it was the fastest way to mount a sprint on the straights, and so you could lop valuable split seconds off your time in any race. There was also a certain amount of slaloming, and riding through and off (passing from the front of a group to the rear), to demonstrate before Courtney signed you off, gave you your spurs. Then you were accredited, licensed and ready to race. I really missed that course when it had finished.

But I was good to go, and being a member of the League of Veteran Racing Cyclists (LVRC) I signed up for its two-day Track Championships, which were held in the late autumn, quite fortuitously, at Newport Velodrome. One raced in one's appropriate age category and I was down to ride in the 60-65 age group.

You would think that these venerable old boys would, at their advanced time of life, settle quite literally for an easy ride and contentedly meander around the track and not bother that much. Not a bit of it! This age group contained past and present world champions, national champions and ex-pro riders, and this melange of riders meant that I was on a hiding to nothing which, in fairness, I usually received. In the races against the clock, it therefore became for me, as always, a matter of setting and attempting to better personal bests for the relevant distances.

The first event I rode in was the sprint which would be a series of two-man head-to-head races, but instead of drawing the order FA Cup-style from a hat, then one was timed over the fastest 200 metres first of all in an individual time trial effort. You were given two and a half laps to gradually build momentum whilst ascending the banking to the very top then, when one received the bell for one's final lap, dramatically descending to hit the 200 metre mark on the sprint line at the bottom of the track at top speed, from where one's effort to the finish line was timed electronically.

The draw for the knockout stages then saw the seeding of the fastest rider in the time trial versus the slowest, then the second fastest against the second slowest and so on. Although I had put in a very creditable and speedy time I was nevertheless the slowest, and was therefore ranged against the quickest; the favourite; the number one seed.

As luck would have it this happened to be the (age group) world champion Steve Davies, from Ferryhill Wheelers in the north east of England. I always seemed to be pitted against Steve, because he was always the quickest, and invariably I wasn't.

The head to head, or match sprints, were over three 250-metre laps of the velodrome, with the first lap as always fought out on a cat-and-mouse basis, sometimes at walking pace, as the riders would jockey for the best tactical position as the bell lap approached.

Neither competitor would want to be the first to break for home and thus hand the initiative to the rider coming from behind to surge down the banking with the requisite momentum, and taking the spoils on the finishing line.

After a couple of, naturally, unsuccessful meetings with Steve, on one occasion I had to decide how best to tactically approach the thankless task of taking on Steve Davies.

I had tried the cat-and-mouse method in a previous contretemps against him, only for him to effortlessly do just enough to beat me on the line, i.e. saving his energy for tougher heats ahead. I had made the tactical error of being the first to make the break on the bell, only to be easily outsprinted and left for dead on the back straight, leaving him again to coast home without breaking sweat.

On this occasion I was being pushed off by Jim Varnish, a member of Halesowen CC, father of Jess Varnish, the Olympic sprinter and erstwhile partner in the Olympic team sprint of Victoria Pendleton.

Jim was a former world champion in another discipline, cycle speedway, so he knew a thing or three about match sprinting. He suggested the way to beat Steve was to go from the gun, surprising him and holding him off for the whole three laps. I thought about this, consulting my brother, who was also competing in this event albeit in the age group above, and he agreed with Jim that this was the way to go.

I didn't agree fully, as I reasoned that I couldn't hold him off for three laps, so mentally I compromised and I decided I would go early with a lap and a half to go, and surprise him by building a big enough lead and then holding him off.

The gun fired, and we did the slow dance for the first lap and a half as planned, then I went for it. Through the bell I surged in a clear lead. Only one lap to hold him off and then I would have served up the shock of the championships.

Down the back straight I powered, glancing over my right shoulder and I couldn't even see him! Around the final bend and I was hugging the sprinter's line which is the shortest route home and we were into the final straight and still I couldn't see him.

The only time I saw him was when he overtook me on the line to win by the width of a tyre. Gallant effort? Nah. Steve knew to the centimetre when to overhaul me, and he just hung me out to dry. But he always had a cheery handshake after the race and sometimes a helpful word of advice. He was in a different class to me, but I had then and still have the utmost respect for him.

My real salutary lesson came in the UCI World Masters Track Championship held at Manchester Velodrome, the home of British Cycling. This is a bona fide World Championship event as it is run and administered by the *Union de Cyclisme Internationale*, cycling's world governing body. Manchester had a virtual monopoly on the event, which meant that us Brits didn't have the expense of getting to somewhere like Perth in Australia or some far-flung South American venue.

The European Championships were held one year in somewhere remote like Georgia, the old Soviet Republic, and I believe the entire French team turned up in one car to find they were virtually the only non-Georgians who could find, let alone reach the place. The results of this Championship unsurprisingly showed a clean sweep of medals to the Georgian team, so having the World Championships in Manchester was an advantage to home riders not to be surrendered easily.

World Championship sounds like a real achievement just to qualify to be involved, but that is not the case, as there is no qualification required; simply an entry fee coupled with one's track accreditation, and you are then good to go.

The calibre of the opposition always matched the event's billing, but more of that anon. I took my place in the sprint time trial and as usual didn't uproot any trees. Therefore in Round One of the match sprint, I was pitted against some bloke with tanned legs from the other side of the planet.

As usual, he put me away with consummate ease and then I found myself in the repechage heat, which was a second chance for all the first-round losers, with the winner of that little shindig being advanced into the second round. But instead of a head-to-head match race, there were four riders in my heat.

Get this! One was the former world record holder, one was the former world champion, another was an ex-Olympian, and then there was me making up the numbers. I can't remember which was which, but there was a German, a South African, a guy from the States and me, Porky on a bike.

Well, I hadn't got a clue how to play this one as the gun started us off. First lap, cat-and-mouse, I crawled to the front and then pulled up high on the banking so that I could keep a watching brief.

Second lap saw more catting and mousing, as we again found ourselves high on the banking approaching the finishing straight ready to take the bell.

My brain suddenly screamed at me to go! I shot down the banking and took the bell on the sprinter's line in the straight with a clear lead. Into the penultimate banking with just 200 metres to glory.

Down the back straight, and then whoosh! My three expert rivals shot past me as one body, and in the space of about two seconds I had been relegated from clear leader to hopeless also-ran.

I chugged down the final straight as the three of them were already shaking hands as they slowed down on the far banking. I don't think they even noticed I had participated in the race. To this date I have never won a match sprint. Little bloody wonder, as tactically I am remedial. Ah well.

One event in which I did have a modicum of success at the World Championships was the Individual Pursuit. This is an event raced against the clock over eight laps, or 2,000 metres of the velodrome. It takes place with two riders on the boards at any one time, starting on opposite straights, and after being held up and pushed off then it is a lung-bursting effort, which frequently does (and should) leave you gasping for oxygen as you cross the finishing line.

I have also suffered in this event from something called "pursuiter's throat" which afflicts competitors such as me whose riding style is mouth open, gulping in air. This leaves you at the conclusion of your effort with a raw throat and a chesty cough, and an annoying inability to be able to clear your throat. This malaise can last for anything up to two or three hours, which can be a major problem as within that timeframe you may be required to go again for a medal run-off race. That latter part was never going to be a problem for me though, let's face it!

However, I did say that I had a little success in the pursuit. One had to submit one's Personal Best time for the event on the entry application form, and this determined the running order with the slowest pair of riders beginning the proceedings in the first heat.

Of course, I was in the first heat and as this was the World Championships, I had a "local derby" against a Scotsman called Jim Robertson.

Now Jim was a real veteran of the world championships, competing for the honour and not the glory, a bit like myself. Jim and I set off on our eight-lap trundle, (it's all relative isn't it – the better riders seem to fly around the track, we mere mortals trundle) and I was quickly into my stride, busting my lungs as the laps ticked by, it seemed, punishingly slowly.

With about a lap and a half to go I shot past Jim, having pursued and caught up the half-lap he had started on the other side of the boards and yours truly crossed the line, victorious in my heat, for a change!

I looked up at the electronic scoreboard to see my time and there I was greeted with the sight of my name, my country and the numeral 1, signifying that at that precise moment I was leading the world championships!

I hastily reached for my mobile phone to take a photo of this momentous achievement before the screen was reconfigured with the riders for the next heat, which I managed, and I have this photo which proudly shows me as leader of the world for that split second!

How many billions of years has the planet existed? This moment was unique in all of that time. "B. Jones GBR 1: J Robertson GBR 2". It had been worth all of the effort and pain just for that single moment! Ha! Take that one away from me, if you dare!!! If the world had ended at that moment then I would have gone to meet my maker as the reigning World Champion. Slap my face and wake me up, please!

With my lack of tactical nous on the track not improving season by season, I then (inadvisedly) entered the World Championship Scratch Race, which was a sixty-lap race around the boards with the first past the post being declared the victor.

60 laps would take about 20 minutes or so and there were about two dozen riders on the line for the start. After a couple of laps spent getting over your gears and picking up a little speed, then the peloton began to form up more meaningfully. 20 or so riders may be quite a sight for the spectators, but when you are out there it involves full concentration as, thinking back to Courtney Rowe's tutelage, one mistake and you are all waiting for an ambulance.

The race unfolds with the peloton stringing out into one long line and lapping the track with a rhythmic cadence. The rider on the front of the bunch would peel off to the top of the banking each half lap, and then drop back down as the last riders shot through underneath him. Thus he would systematically take his place at the rear of the peloton and start to gradually work his way back to the front of the string.

This manoeuvre means that the pace of the peloton can be maintained, and no individual rider has to shoulder all the workload, which is shared equally until the hammer goes down.

When it came to my turn to hit the front I was ready. The first half lap arrived and I felt good. My asses ears must have been protruding from under my helmet by now, because I felt even better after one full lap in the lead! I thought "This will show them what I am made of!", so I did two full laps as my turn on the front before finally pulling over wearily to the top of the banking.

This was where my tactical knowhow let me down badly. As the peloton shot through underneath me, I duly dropped down only to see the last rider disappear into the distance with the rest of the peloton in front of him.

I didn't have the legs even to jump onto the rear of the string, and within a couple of circuits I had been lapped and very shortly after lapped again. To hide my exhaustion and embarrassment I quickly abandoned the race, and retired to the inner to lick my injured pride.

Bless him, Steve Davies came up to me after the race and gently advised me that everyone always does just a half lap on the front as their turn, and then you haven't burned you boats stamina-wise. The idea is to bide your time in the peloton, storing up your energy; and then when the balloon finally does go up then you have enough in the tank to respond.

If I keep riding by the time I am about 120, I may have learnt all the lessons the hard way to make me remotely competitive on the track.

Stamina at that age would be the main stumbling block, I would imagine!

Whilst I was training for one World Championship event on the outdoor track at Halesowen I was involved in a terrific pile up, which left me battered and extremely bruised.

We were involved in a team pursuit training discipline and I was in a line of five riders, some of whom were young (but talented nonetheless) teenagers. The front rider pulls up on the banking each half lap and drops down to the back of the line, as with the scratch race in the preceding paragraph.

When it came to my turn I duly pulled up the banking and dropped down, only to "feather" the back wheel of the boy on the back of the line. A touch of wheels, no matter how slight, will bring both riders down, and down we came at top speed. As I was cleated it into my pedals I remained attached to my bike. Falling to my left towards the track infield, I did a complete somersault, bounced and did another punishing forward roll before coming to rest on my left side.

I was wearing a brand-new helmet and I felt it scrape along the tarmac during this awful crash, but this probably saved me from stowing the side of my head in. I had taken all the skin off my left side from armpit to ankle, and my Lycra skinsuit was torn from my body, revealing lumps of bloodied and raw flesh. I remained conscious the whole time but felt no reason to move from my prone position on the track inner.

I could hear the sound of shocked voices getting nearer and footsteps pounding, urging me and whoever else had come down in this melee not to move. I was quite happy to obey this instruction. After ascertaining that I was still breathing and was indeed still conscious, I was eventually lifted to my feet and escorted, oh so gingerly, back to the starting line where all our gear was.

When one suffers injuries like this it sometimes takes some time before the pain and the stiffness takes hold. I was therefore able to walk to a car where my tangled bike and I were safely ensconced to be driven home, as I had ridden to the track that night and would have ridden home after training.

Before continuing with this tale, I will hold my hands up and admit responsibility for the crash, as it was my wheel which touched the other rider and brought him down. This was not through my negligence; more a case of the slight misjudgement which can cause a calamitous outcome such as this.

The major problem with this was that it was the Thursday night before the LVRC Track Championships started at Newport only 36 hours later at Newport. Like a good'un, I duly registered to participate on the following Saturday morning, swathed in plasters and bandages and as stiff as an ironing board. I got through that two-day event. (I don't know how. Am I tougher than I think?)

I then pressed on with my training as the UCI World Championship was but 14 days hence. Again I presented myself for registration at Manchester Velodrome. My injuries had subsided to the point where the only outwardly-visible sign of my previous misfortune was my left arm, which was bandaged rather crudely with about three miles of gauze held in place by a strip of Elastoplast (other plasters are available).

The UCI Track Masters Championships, like the LVRC Track Championships, have a full complement of St John's Ambulance staff on duty, for very obvious reasons. Whilst passing their makeshift waiting room at the side of the track I was called in by one of the medics.

He wanted to have a look at what was underneath this Heath Robinson bandage and he recoiled in horror as he stripped it down to my flesh.

He informed me that it wasn't healing properly (as my Mom would have said, it was going bad ways) and it would need him to expertly re-dress it, and I would have to have a course of antibiotics to fight any infection.

I was also told in no uncertain terms that if I carried on to compete then it was at my own responsibility, because he would recommend that I should scratch (if you will pardon the pun) from the whole event. I thanked him for his advice and care, and decided that I would compete, as the nutjob inside me couldn't stomach the waste of money from my entry fees, hotels bills and petrol costs if I didn't race. So I raced; I didn't win anything, I didn't improve my tactical nous, but I was happy.

Competing in the World Championships against riders from all four corners of the globe (is that an expression propagated by the Flat Earth Society, as geographically a globe can't have any corners!) meant that one speaks to some interesting characters.

Once, I got talking to a guy from the States as we were queueing up to get on the track for a warm-up session one morning, and the conversation got round to what we do for a living. I was, at the time, quite uninterestingly, an Independent Financial Advisor, which wouldn't seduce any of the Bond girls away from 007 due to its sheer unsexiness; and he told me that he built indoor velodromes!

Now that, in my book IS pretty damned sexy. He said he had built one in the New York area and was now working on another in California. I am not sure if he was as in awe of me for arranging pension plans, life cover and ISA investments as I was of him. I suspect not.

Finally, if I haven't said it before, I firmly believe that riding on the track is the most fun one can have on a bike. I will get back to it soon, probably once I have had my 70th birthday, as I will once again be the youngest in my age group, and logically, at my most competitive. Watch this space!

CHAPTER FOURTEEN

Coronavirus

As I put the finishing touches to this book, we are in the grip of what seems to be the early stages of the Coronavirus, or Covid-19 pandemic in the United Kingdom. It has been memorably described by one of the Government's scientific advisers as "Round One of this Pandemic".

We watch and listen with trepidation to the daily press conferences broadcast live on the television by our Prime Minister Boris Johnson, his trusted medical advisers and the measures being put in place by the new Chancellor of the Exchequer Rishi Sunak, the Secretary of State for Health Matt Hancock, and the Foreign Secretary Dominic Raab. Indeed, Raab had to stand in for the Prime Minister as he battled for his life in intensive care having succumbed to the virus.

Boris himself I am sure shocked the nation by succumbing to the virus himself, and spending that anxious time in intensive care. He survived, thankfully, whatever your political persuasion, but not before he brought home the gravity of the situation.

What it all means to us is that our lives have changed completely in a few short days, and possibly permanently. My own job as a Bikeability Instructor has been suspended due to the indefinite closure of all schools, and we are all urged to respect one another with social distancing.

Pubs, restaurants, schools are closed, and all sporting activities and social gatherings are now prohibited, not by law, not yet, but by the PM's appeal to common sense. We were in the throes of panic buying in the supermarkets of items such as toilet rolls (?), hand sanitiser, soap, bread, eggs; this list is becoming exhaustive, although things have stabilised somewhat. We are all being urged to stay at home for the weeks, even months to come. No one in our lifetime has experienced anything remotely like this.

God continues with his work and we still have the pleasure of seeing the season of spring change the natural world, albeit mostly through our windows, and I for one have always found this to be the most wonderful time of year, as everything wakes from its winter hibernation. It is a time of renewal, both naturally and spiritually as we approach Eastertide. But this year, and possibly next year, it will all be different. Life has to, and will, go on; and my relentless optimism for life will help me face whatever befalls me.

For now, I am getting out on my bike as before. Riding alone I can observe social distancing whilst being safe in the fresh air that God has provided for us. Cycling is an allowable form of exercise once a day, as are walking or jogging.

As my time trials, in common with all official sporting events, have been cancelled pending further advice, I have taken it upon myself to ride the races that I would have ridden, but on my own. Observing everything that I would do for a normal race, I put my race head on and go out and simply ride the races. This will keep me fit for when racing resumes, but just as importantly, as I am in my 70th year, my fitness will, God willing, help me to combat this dreadful virus should I be unfortunate enough to succumb.

If the day comes when we are forbidden to go outdoors then I will continue riding (and simulating racing) on my rollers in the kitchen.

I cannot add any more at the moment, as who knows what the weeks and months ahead have in store for us. But my bicycle will remain my staunchest ally as we strive to come safely out of this terrible period in our history.

God be with us.

CONCLUSION

Embracing cycling in the way I have has given me the strength and will to ride on any day of the year, regardless of the vagaries of the British climate, which as we all know, can be unforgiving and downright challenging at any time of the calendar. Christmas Day to me is not an excuse to have a day off and not ride.

The festive period is difficult enough without all the food and confectionery on offer, but I always get up and out, or if the weather is inclement, then I do a meaningful session on the rollers. In this way, I have earned my Christmas dinner, and I can pig out in the knowledge that I have already burnt sufficient calories for the day's excesses not to cause me problems. Obsessive? You bet your life!

I visited the battlefields of the First World War in northern France and Belgium in 2018, and was made aware of the huge contribution that cyclists made to the war effort on those very killing fields. This I found extremely moving and I venerate the memories of these men and their machines. I am a pacifist at heart. but if I had been compelled to fight for my King and country then I would have loved to have been one of those soldiers on bicycles who helped to turn that awful conflict in our favour. And I remember those who perished while they were doing so. God bless you all, and I hope your proud descendants became cyclists.

The four seasons, or *les quatre saisons* to express it in the mother tongue of the UCI, mean different things to me. I am going to discuss them in chronological order, but I will begin with summer.

This is the season of long daylight hours; warm, even hot weather, and the height of the time trial calendar, when I can be knocking out five, six or even seven races a week. Especially the midweek time trials where I ride to and from the venues are so enjoyable, because

I might ride home afterwards, getting there at about 9.30 p.m. when the sun is still shining. In Surrey and Sussex, where time appears to have stood still in the villages for at least the last fifty years or so these evenings are idyllic and I treasure them. It can be cold and very wet as well in a UK summer, but this time of year has many advantages and benefits.

Autumn, however, fills me with sadness and foreboding. Sadness, because it heralds the end of our beloved summer, and the beginning of the end of the time trialling season. I do not stand in the camp of those who proclaim this particular season to be the loveliest of all because of its variety of colours. To me it is the slow death of the leaves and greenery and all the natural life that made midsummer so wistfully beautiful. The days begin to get shorter, and quite rapidly. There is a chill in the air, which is the precursor of those long, miserable winter days and nights that lie in store for us. Riding around on the bike in autumn means putting on extra layers to combat the falling temperatures.

Winter, ah yes, winter. In the UK winters are uniformly grey, uniformly wet and uniformly miserable. Daylight hours seem to be rationed, temperatures usually refuse to be anything other than unpleasant, and road conditions for cycling can range from frozen, and by definition, treacherous, to flooded, and by the same definition, even more treacherous.

We don't even seem to have the fun release of the frequent snowfalls we seemed to get all the time when I was a nipper. No, you can keep autumn as far as I am concerned, colours and all, and don't get me started on winter! Not my cup of tea.

I firmly believe that these days the seasons are all merging into one, and the only way you can tell what time of year it is in the UK if you have suddenly arrived from Outer Space is whether or not there are leaves on the trees. On the many days when it is not possible to get out on the bike due to the lousy weather conditions, then you have to get your pedalling fix indoors, whether on the turbo trainer, the rollers or the static bike. Winter, in my book, lasts an eternity. It always seems to be winter in the UK, and as I get older I seem to spend my life pining for the summer preceded by the advent of spring.

Now Spring, that is my favourite season. It heralds the ending of winter and the approach of summer. To me it is the antithesis of autumn, where everything is starting to die off, it is when nature renews its promise to Mother Earth and the daylight hours begin joyously to lengthen.

It also means that the time trialling season is getting underway, and there are several months of racing to look forward to for addicts lie me. Whenever the first crocus pokes its pretty little colourful head out of the soil, I automatically switch from the winter miserabilist that I have become and morph into the spring-loving fanatic that is now a part of my psyche.

Spring has become everything to me, and as a cyclist, the pleasure I get from riding around in the improving conditions, when the weather is better, the roads are more rideable and one can leave off all the additional layers of waterproof and heat-retaining paraphernalia that one has been forced to wear, is immeasurable.

The moon is 238,000 miles from the Earth. At the time of writing I have ridden over 138,000 miles so I am well over halfway there. At my current rate of progress I want to "reach" the moon by my 80th birthday. Who is to say I won't achieve this? The bicycle has enabled me to dream, and above all else, enabled me to achieve.

And if I do reach the moon, what then? I'll tell you what, I will simply carry on riding and reach for the stars. I have an ambition to join the "300" club, that is exclusive to those who have ridden 300,000 miles. Again, my current rate of progress means I am unlikely to hit that figure before my 85th birthday, but I will be getting there, make no mistake, God willing.

There is a chap from Surrey who in 2019 became the first Brit to ride one million miles, and he is about 90 years old and has been in the saddle since 1951. I will not live long enough to equal that feat, but what an achievement is his. Chapeau sir!

When I peg it, please bury me in lycra, in Wolverhampton Wanderers colours, and then I can start cycling in heaven. Until then, if you see me on the thoroughfares on my bike, give me a wave and just think "Good on, yer Joner!".

On my bike I am in a world of my own. If I am not striving to get up a hill or thundering along a flat section at top speed in a high gear, then I am not happy. Please don't misunderstand me in that cycling is a substitute for human relationships, most definitely it is not.

I understand life's priorities. But this is my hobby, my passion, my sport. And all this I believe will help me to stay fit, healthy, supple and young. And above all, fight off all the illnesses and conditions which could shorten my life or make me lose my dignity.

Ladies and gentlemen, I sincerely hope that I have presented to you the bicycle in all its glory. It is one of the greatest inventions of recent generations, and its contribution to the health and wellbeing of this planet's inhabitants is immeasurable. Without the bicycle we would undoubtedly all be far worse off. Our physiology owes an incalculable debt to the bicycle.

My dotage will continue to be misspent, but, after all the evidence I have presented to the contrary in the previous pages, *is* it being misspent? Is it *really*?

You will have to decide for yourself, but I will tell you something, if you want to misspend your own personal dotage, then you won't find a better way of doing it! Believe me, having discovered cycling at the tender age of 56-and-three-quarters, I wish I had followed in my brother's teenage footsteps and taken up the sport and stuck at it.

I was a decently good footballer and a cricketer who enjoyed some exceptional success on the fields of play at both sports, and I would have swapped all of that for a career as a racing cyclist.

Who knows how good I could have become? When I sit down with my Maker, I think I will make a polite enquiry and seek an answer to that last question I posed.

God has seen fit to bless me with the ability to ride a bike and I hope I can use this gift until I get my card from the Queen (or rather King, as it will be in the year 2050). When I am finally called home on my own personal day of judgment and I stand before St Peter as he vets me for the pearly gates, when he asks me to state my earthly occupation I shall have just the one-word answer for him.

Cyclist.

Happy cycling, everyone!